Traditional Quilts
to Paper Piece

Traditional Quilts
to Paper Piece

14 SMALL PROJECTS

Cori Derksen and Myra Harder

Martingale®
& COMPANY

Traditional Quilts to Paper Piece: 14 Small Projects
© 2003 Cori Derksen and Myra Harder

That Patchwork Place® is an imprint of
Martingale & Company®.

Martingale & Company
20205 144th Avenue NE
Woodinville, WA 98072-8478
www.martingale-pub.com

Mission Statement
Dedicated to providing quality products
and service to inspire creativity.

Credits

President . . . . Nancy J. Martin
CEO . . . . Daniel J. Martin
Publisher . . . . Jane Hamada
Editorial Director . . . . Mary V. Green
Managing Editor . . . . Tina Cook
Technical Editor . . . . Dawn Anderson
Copy Editor . . . . Karen Koll
Design Director . . . . Stan Green
Illustrator . . . . Robin Strobel
Cover Designer . . . . Regina Girard
Text Designer . . . . Jennifer LaRock Shontz
Photographer . . . . Brent Kane

Printed in China
08 07 06 05 04 03   8 7 6 5 4 3 2 1

Library of Congress Cataloging-in-Publication Data
   Derksen, Cori.
      Traditional quilts to paper piece / Cori Derksen
and Myra Harder.
      ISBN 1-56477-478-3
   1. Patchwork–Patterns. 2. Machine quilting–Patterns.
I. Harder, Myra. II. Title.
      TT835 .D464 2003
      746.46'041—dc21
                                                2002153994

Dedication

This book is dedicated to the many friends we have made along the way. We are very grateful to have a local quilt guild called the Barnswallows. Its members continually amaze us with their creations. To the quilters of southern Manitoba who have taught us, inspired us, and encouraged us: we thank you!

Acknowledgments

Our sincere thanks and appreciation go to the many friends and family who gave time and skills so that we could share our designs:

    Betty Klassen, for all the machine quilting

    Our friends:

        Bonnie Hildebrand—Winnipeg, Manitoba

        Bev DeRoo—Swan Lake, Manitoba

        Laura Kotschorek—Somerset, Manitoba

        Andrea Fehr—Winkler, Manitoba

        Sally Unrau—Morden, Manitoba

        Pearl Braun-Dyck—Plum Coulee, Manitoba

    Our photographer, Marlene Lindal

Contents

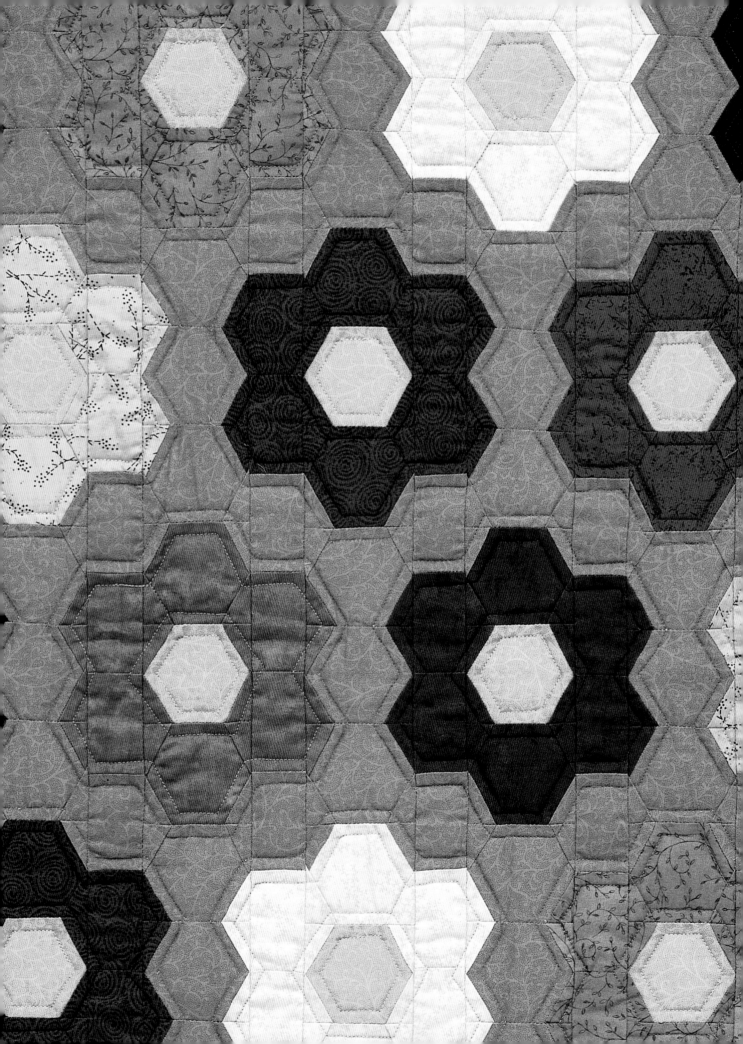

Introduction

Traditional Quilts to Paper Piece is a collection of traditional quilts with a twist. We wanted to provide an option for the quilter who likes the traditional look but prefers a method that is easier and faster than piecing with traditional templates. Some of the quilts in this book come from our design archives, some are quilts that we have made for ourselves, and others are new off the drawing board. We have designed all of the quilts with the goal of keeping the traditional versions in mind while giving the old designs a new and fresh feeling. We have also chosen many different color combinations and hope that you feel free to use still others if you wish. A different color can change the whole feeling of a piece.

Getting Started

FOUNDATION CHOICES

Cori explains paper piecing as simply "sewing by number." To help you better understand the process, look at one of the block patterns found with each project. These patterns are transferred onto a paper foundation; then pieces of fabric are sewn to the foundation in the order indicated on the pattern. This method of piecing is simple and fun and produces very accurate results. Traditionally, the three following different foundation materials have been used.

Muslin

In recent years paper piecing has become popular, but the concept of sewing onto a foundation is quite old. Many Crazy quilts from the last century were constructed using a thin fabric such as muslin for the foundation. A foundation helped to stabilize odd-shaped quilt pieces cut from a variety of fabrics. When muslin was used as a foundation, any planned design was drawn onto the foundation by hand. The quilter worked with the pattern facing up and simply sewed and flipped the pieces as she went along. The muslin foundation remained behind the block, giving the quilt additional warmth and eliminating the need for batting. This method made the quilt top quite thick and therefore it was tied, rather than hand quilted.

Interfacing and Stabilizers

Interfacing and stabilizers are other foundation options. There are many varieties on the market; some must remain behind the block and others can be torn away, brushed off, or dissolved with water. Any interfacing or stabilizer used as a foundation must be strong enough so the pattern can be drawn on it without distorting it or tearing it. It should also be thin if you intend to leave it behind the finished block, or, if you plan to remove it, it should be easy to remove without ripping out stitches. Note that any foundation left behind the pieced block becomes a permanent part of the project, making hand quilting difficult.

Paper

In today's world of foundation piecing, paper is the most commonly used foundation and the one we used for all of the quilts in this book. It is an inexpensive and disposable foundation that offers some advantages that muslin and interfacing cannot. Patterns can be easily duplicated on a photocopier or even printed from your home computer, rather than hand drawn onto the foundation. In addition, paper is less expensive than muslin or interfacing, easy to see through, and easy to remove from the finished block. There are papers made specifically for paper piecing; however, they are optional. Simply look for a paper that is easy to see through and to tear away. This method differs from using muslin or interfacing foundations in that with paper foundations, the quilter works with the pattern face down, so the final image is a mirror image of the original design.

FABRIC CHOICES

Because the quilts in this book are relatively small, you may be able to use up some of the scraps in your collection. Whether you are buying new fabrics or using what you have, here are a few things to consider about your fabric choices for paper piecing.

Cotton

We love cotton! We find cotton to be the least frustrating of all fabrics, and final projects made with cotton are quite rewarding. Besides, there are so many beautiful cotton prints and plaids available that it is hard not to be drawn to them. When using a foundation, it is possible to mix and match different types of fabrics; however, we still feel you will get the best results if you use the same fabric type throughout your quilt. Polyester-cotton blends work, but they tend to be a little transparent, and velvets, polyesters, and silks can shift while sewing. Also, history has proved that cotton quilts will last for many generations, so if you want future generations to enjoy your handiwork, we recommend using cotton.

Checks and Plaids

Sometimes the direction the print runs on a block doesn't matter, but with patterns such as checks and plaids, the entire block may look crooked if you don't stitch along one of the printed lines. If you choose to use checks and plaids, stitch them to your foundation carefully, stitching on one of the printed lines or parallel to one of the printed lines in the fabric (see "Flying Dutchman" on page 48). Another option is to reserve your checks and plaids for sashings, borders, and bindings where straight strips are used so you don't have to worry about how the pattern will look when pieced at odd angles.

Print Size

When choosing prints, keep in mind the project that you are working on and the size of pieces that you are working with. You may walk into your favorite quilt shop and fall in love with a beautiful, big, floral print. Buy it if you want to, but save it for another project. With paper piecing you will want to use smaller prints. If you use large prints when piecing smaller blocks, the final look will be unattractive, and it will be more difficult to recognize the finished design. You can still use floral prints in these projects, but use small-scale florals in the blocks and save the large, bold prints for borders or backings.

Fabric Grain Line

When we are paper piecing, we give very little thought to the direction of the fabric grain line. Because we are working with small fabric pieces that will be stabilized by the foundation paper, very little shifting or stretching will occur in the block. Only when we are paper piecing blocks 6" and larger with eight or fewer pieces do we consider that the fabric grain line may have some impact on the block (because the fabrics may shift and distort the shape of the block).

For added stability, keep the paper foundation on the block until you have joined the blocks in the project.

REPRODUCING BLOCK PATTERNS

The easiest way to reproduce the block patterns in this book is to photocopy them. In the past, many photocopy machines would distort the shape or size of the block pattern; the photocopiers that we use today are much more accurate. It is still wise to test any photocopy machine for accuracy and quality. The easiest way to know if the machine is accurate is to print a simple square block and then hold it up to the light to compare it to your original. The two blocks should line up. Always make copies from your original pattern and not from another photocopy, because copying from a copy can compound the distortion factor.

Another option is to trace the block patterns onto the foundation material. Use a ruler for accuracy and be sure to transfer the numbers that relate to the piecing sequence. You must use this method when using muslin, interfacing, or a stabilizer as foundation material.

TIP A great way to adjust the size of any of the quilts in this book is to reduce or enlarge the block patterns on a photocopier. This way you can customize the size of a quilt to fit a specific spot in your home. If you choose to reduce or enlarge any of the patterns, just be sure to check that the block patterns aren't distorted in the process.

Paper-Piecing Instructions

The block patterns for the quilts in this book are located with the instructions for each project. Each block is either a single unit or is made up of multiple units that will need to be pieced together to make the block. Patterns for single-unit blocks have a dark, solid line around them. Patterns for multiple-unit blocks are presented in several sections; each section has a dark, solid line around it.

Each block pattern, whether it's made up of a single unit or multiple units, has several pieces. The pieces are numbered in the order they are to be sewn. To paper piece the blocks, follow these steps.

1. Transfer the number of block patterns needed for each project onto the desired foundation material. Cut out single-unit block patterns along the dark solid line that runs around the pattern's outer edges. Cut multiple-unit block patterns apart along

each dark, solid line. Keep in mind that the pattern is the finished size of the block, so the fabric pieces along the outer edges will need to extend at least ¼" beyond the foundation to act as your seam allowance.

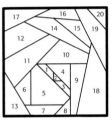 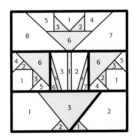

Single-Unit Block Multiple-Unit Block

2. Set your sewing machine's stitch length for 15 to 18 stitches per inch. Insert a size 90/14 needle into the machine. If the paper foundation tears away as you sew, decrease the number of stitches per inch; if the

HELPFUL HINTS

The following are just a few little hints that we have picked up along the way. We hope they will make paper piecing more enjoyable for you.

- Keep any excess threads trimmed short because they love to get into your machine and jam things up.
- If using regular photocopy paper as a foundation, lightly mist the paper with water before tearing it off. This makes it easier to remove and less likely to rip out your stitches.
- Always cut the largest pieces of fabric first; then cut up the remaining fabric for paper piecing.
- Always press the completed units before joining them into blocks.
- Insert a pin along your intended sewing line on the front side of the pattern. Then when you turn your pattern over to lay down the next piece of fabric you will have a seam allowance guide to assist you in positioning the fabric.

stitches loosen up as you pull the foundation away, increase the number of stitches per inch. It is unnecessary to backstitch because the closeness of the stitches keeps the pieces from pulling apart.

3. Place each unit of the pattern in front of you with the marked side facing up. This will be referred to as the pattern right side. The unmarked side will be referred to as the wrong side. Remember that once your block is completed it will be a mirror image of the original pattern.

4. For each unit, cut a piece of fabric for the piece marked 1. Refer to the project photos for guidance in choosing fabrics. Be sure the piece of fabric is at least ¼" larger all the way around than the size of the piece it will cover. Do not attempt to cut the fabric to size. Just be sure the fabric amply covers the piece; the excess will be trimmed away later.

5. Hold the unit up to a light with the printed side facing you. Place the wrong side of fabric piece 1 on the wrong side of the pattern so it covers piece 1. Temporarily pin the piece in place. When you hold the unit up to the light, piece 1 should be entirely covered by the fabric.

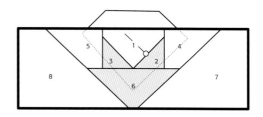

6. Cut a piece of fabric at least ⅜" larger all the way around than piece 2.

7. Hold the unit up to a light with the right side of the block facing you. Place fabric piece 2 over fabric piece 1, right sides together, with at least ¼" of fabric extending over the line that separates pieces 1 and 2.

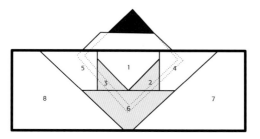

8. Working on the right side of the pattern, sew along the thin black line that separates pieces 1 and 2.

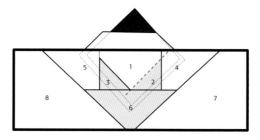

9. Fold back piece 2 along the seam line. Hold the unit up to the light. Be sure that pieces 1 and 2 are covered and that the fabric piece for each piece extends at least ¼" on all sides.

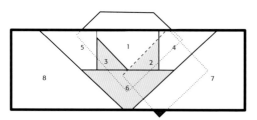

10. Working on the pattern wrong side, fold piece 2 back up so the fabric wrong side is facing up. Trim the seam allowance between pieces 1 and 2 to ¼". If the excess fabric isn't trimmed away, it can eventually build up and make quilting more difficult later.

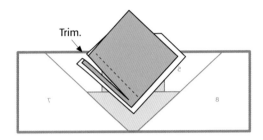

Trim.

11. Fold piece 2 down. Finger-press or use a wood pressing tool to press the seam allowance flat.

12. Continue adding fabric pieces in numerical order in the same manner.

13. When you have added all of the fabric pieces to each block or unit, lightly press each block or unit and trim the outer seam allowances to ¼".

14. If you are piecing a multiple-unit block, stitch the units together so they are a mirror image of the block pattern. Remember—the finished block is a mirror image of the pattern. Lightly press the block.

15. Remove the foundations as instructed for each project.

TIP To join two angled units of a multiple-unit block, first place the right sides of the units together. Then push a positioning pin through a point from the wrong side of piece 1. Insert the pin through the corresponding point of piece 2. Repeat with a second positioning pin for a second point. Once both positioning pins have been inserted through both pieces and points, secure the pins by bringing them back up through piece 2 and piece 1. Stitch the seam, joining the two pieces.

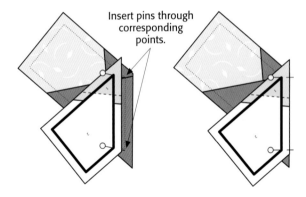

Insert pins through corresponding points.

Quilt Projects

By Myra Harder and Betty Klassen. Quilted by Betty Klassen.

This unique and elegant piece has been on our drawing board for many years; finally we have it completed.

Carolina Lily

FINISHED QUILT SIZE: 38½" X 48½"

MATERIALS

42"-wide fabric

1⅞ yds. of dark plum print for blocks, middle border, outer border, and binding

1⅜ yds. of gold print for blocks, inner border, and middle border

⅞ yd. of navy print for blocks and inner border

¾ yd. of green print for blocks and inner border

¼ yd. of dark blue print for flowerpot

6" strip of dark green print for stems

2½ yds. of fabric for backing

43" x 53" piece of batting

CUTTING INSTRUCTIONS

All measurements include ¼"-wide seam allowances. Cut the borders and largest pieces first, and then use the remaining fabrics for paper piecing.

From the green print, cut:
   10 rectangles, 3" x 5½"
   4 squares, 3" x 3"
From the dark plum print, cut:
   2 strips, 3½" x 42½" from the lengthwise grain
   2 strips, 3½" x 38½"
   4 squares, 1½" x 1½"

ASSEMBLING THE QUILT

1. Using the Carolina Lily patterns on pages 22–23, transfer 18 flower blocks, 17 alternate blocks, 14 inner-border units, and 14 middle-border units to the desired foundation material.

2. Refer to "Paper-Piecing Instructions" on pages 13–15 to construct the following blocks and units.

Light Flower Block
Make 12.

Dark Flower Block
Make 6.

Alternate Block
Make 17.

Inner Border Unit
Make 14.

Middle Border Unit
Make 14.

3. Join the Flower and alternate blocks in 7 rows of 5 blocks each as shown. Join the rows.

4. Join 3 inner-border units, 2 green rectangles, and 2 green squares as shown to make the top and bottom inner-border strips. Join 4 inner-border units and 3 green rectangles to make the side inner-border strips. Press seam allowances away from the paper-pieced units.

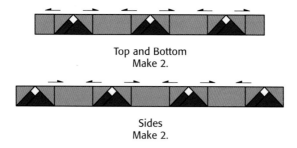

Top and Bottom
Make 2.

Sides
Make 2.

Stitch the side inner-border strips to the sides of the quilt top first; then stitch the top and bottom inner-border strips to the top and bottom edges. Press seam allowances toward the borders.

5. Join 3 middle-border units and 2 plum squares to make the top and bottom middle-border strips. Join 4 middle-border units to make the side middle-border strips.

Top and Bottom
Make 2.

Sides
Make 2.

Stitch the side middle-border strips to the sides of the quilt top first; then stitch the top and bottom middle-border strips to the top and bottom edges. Press seam allowances toward the borders.

6. Referring to "Straight-Cut Borders" on page 87, stitch the 42½" plum outer-border strips to the sides of the quilt top. Stitch the 38½" plum outer-border strips to the top and bottom edges.

7. Remove the paper foundations.

FINISHING THE QUILT

Refer to "Finishing Techniques" on pages 87–93.

1. Layer the quilt top with batting and backing; baste. Quilt as desired.

2. Trim the batting and backing even with the quilt-top edges. Add a hanging sleeve if desired.

3. Make a continuous strip of binding totaling 184" (see "Binding" on page 90). Bind the edges of the quilt and add a label.

COLOR VARIATIONS

PRETTY IN PINK
Brighten up this traditional design,
and think of spring!

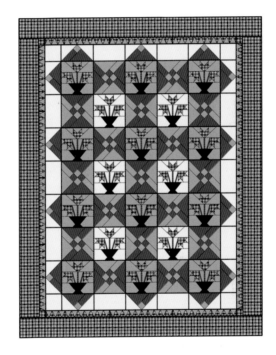

COUNTRY LILY
Through use of rustic plaids and muted colors,
the Carolina Lily takes on a warm country feel.

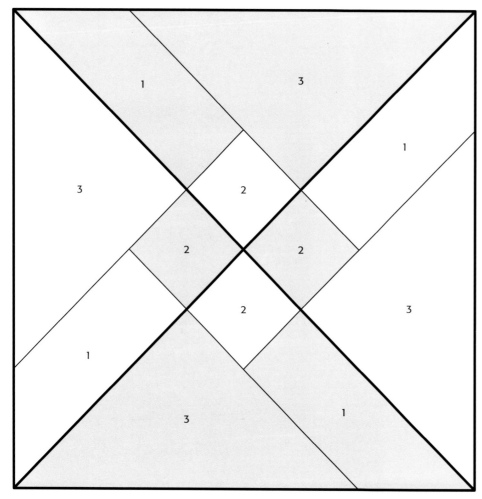

Alternate Block
5" x 5"

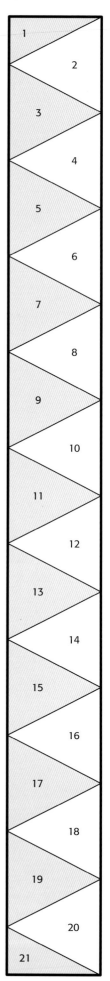

Middle-Border Unit
10" x 1"

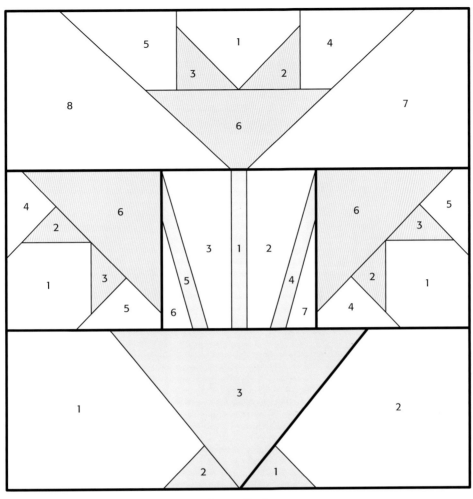

Flower Block
5" x 5"

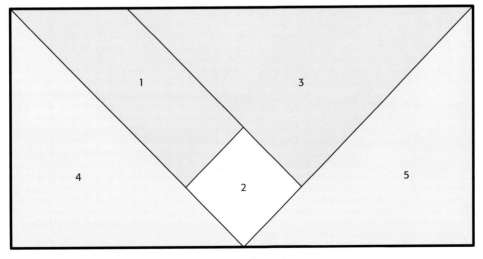

Inner-Border Unit
2½" x 5"

By Bonnie Hildebrand. Quilted by Betty Klassen.
This pineapple quilt makes a great wall hanging and can also be used as a table runner.

Pineapple

FINISHED QUILT SIZE: 27½" x 41½"

MATERIALS

42"-wide fabric

⅞ yd. of gold print for blocks and inner border

⅞ yd. of dark green print for blocks and binding

⅝ yd. of rust print for blocks

⅝ yd. of tan print for blocks

½ yd. of medium green print for blocks and outer border

1½ yds. of fabric for backing

32" x 46" piece of batting

CUTTING INSTRUCTIONS

All measurements include ¼"-wide seam allowances. Cut the borders and largest pieces first, and then use the remaining fabrics for paper piecing.

From the gold print, cut:
- 2 strips, 2½" x 21½"
- 2 strips, 2½" x 39½"

From the medium green print, cut:
- 2 strips, 1½" x 25½"
- 2 strips, 1½" x 41½"

ASSEMBLING THE QUILT

1. Using the Pineapple block pattern on page 27, transfer 15 blocks to the desired foundation material.

2. Refer to "Paper-Piecing Instructions" on pages 13–15 to construct the following blocks.

Make 4.

Make 4.

Make 2.

Make 2.

Make 2.

Make 1.

25

3. Arrange the blocks in 5 rows of 3 blocks each as shown. Join the blocks in rows. Join the rows.

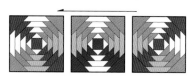

4. Referring to "Straight-Cut Borders" on page 87, stitch the short gold strips to the top and bottom of the quilt top; then stitch the long gold strips to the sides. Repeat with the medium green strips.

5. Remove the paper foundations.

FINISHING THE QUILT

Refer to "Finishing Techniques" on pages 87–93.

1. Layer the quilt top with batting and backing; baste. Quilt as desired.

2. Trim the batting and backing even with the quilt-top edges. Add a hanging sleeve if desired.

3. Make a continuous strip of binding totaling 148" (see "Binding" on page 90). Bind the edges of the quilt and add a label.

COLOR VARIATION

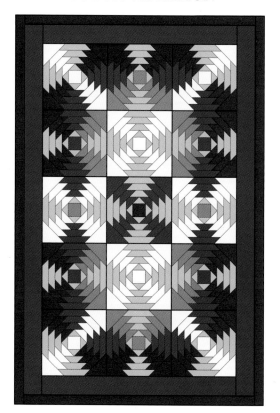

A CHRISTMAS PINEAPPLE

Changing the colors to classic red and green gives you a wall hanging for the holiday season.

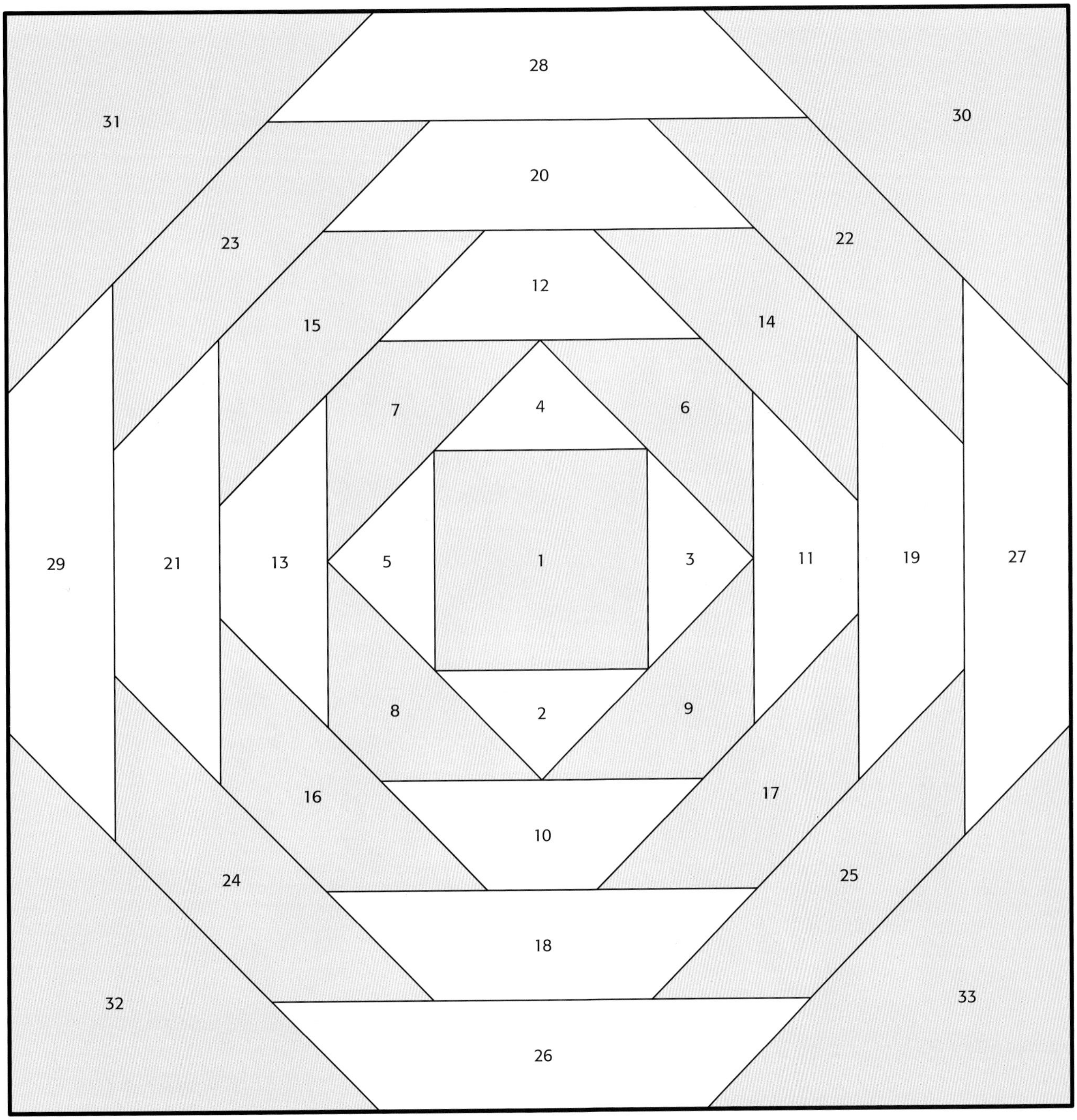

28

31

30

20

23

22

12

15

14

7 4 6

29 21 13 5 1 3 11 19 27

8 2 9

16 17

10

24 25

18

32 33

26

Pineapple Block
7" x 7"

By Cori Derksen. Quilted by Betty Klassen.
Our intention with this design was to create a wall hanging with a masculine look,
to hang in the office of Myra's father.

Hunter's Star

MATERIALS

42"-wide fabric

1 yd. of dark green print for blocks, inner border, corner squares, and binding

¾ yd. of light green print for block backgrounds

½ yd. of green leaf print for blocks and outer border

1⅛ yds. of fabric for backing

39" x 39" piece of batting

CUTTING INSTRUCTIONS

All measurements include ¼"-wide seam allowances. Cut the borders and largest pieces first, and then use the remaining fabric for paper piecing.

From the dark green print, cut:

    2 strips, 1½" x 24½"

    2 strips, 1½" x 26½"

    4 squares, 4½" x 4½"

From the green leaf print, cut:

    4 strips, 4½" x 26½"

ASSEMBLING THE QUILT

1. Using the Hunter's Star patterns on page 31, transfer 36 blocks to the desired foundation material.

2. Refer to "Paper-Piecing Instructions" on pages 13–15 to construct the Hunter's Star blocks.

Hunter's Star Block
Make 36.

3. Arrange the blocks in 6 rows of 6 blocks each as shown. Sew the blocks together in horizontal rows. Join the rows.

4. Referring to "Straight-Cut Borders" on page 87, stitch the short dark green inner-border strips to the sides of the quilt top first; then stitch the long dark green inner-border strips to the top and bottom edges. Referring to "Borders with Corner Squares" on page 87, stitch green leaf-print outer-border strips to the sides of the quilt top. Sew a dark green square to each end of the remaining green leaf-print outer-border strips; press seams toward the border strips. Stitch the strips to the top and bottom edges of the quilt top.

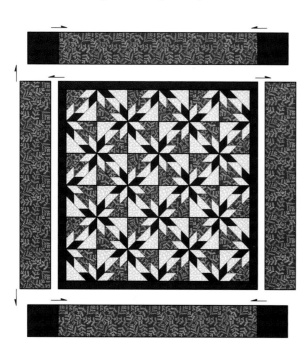

5. Remove the paper foundations.

FINISHING THE QUILT

Refer to "Finishing Techniques" on pages 87–93.

1. Layer the quilt top with batting and backing; baste. Quilt as desired.

2. Trim the batting and backing even with the quilt-top edges. Add a hanging sleeve if desired.

3. Make a continuous strip of binding totaling 148" (see "Binding" on page 90). Bind the edges of the quilt and add a label.

COLOR VARIATION

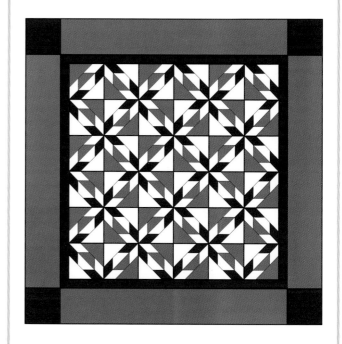

SEASON'S GREETINGS

Using three high-contrast colors, as in this Christmas color scheme, makes stars much more prominent.

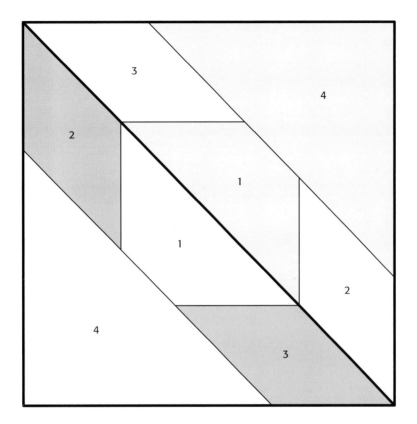

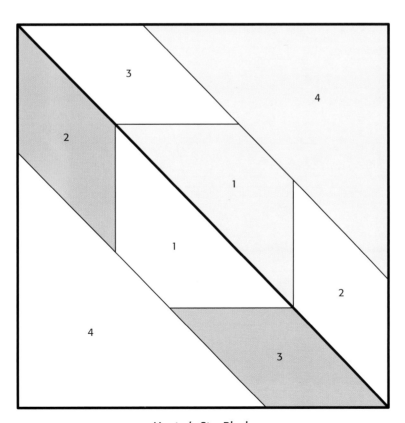

Hunter's Star Blocks
4" x 4"

By Sally Unrau. Quilted by Betty Klassen.
This quilt is a fun variation of the traditional Crazy Patch quilt.

Crazy Patch

FINISHED QUILT SIZE: 30¾" X 37¾"

MATERIALS

42"-wide fabric

1⅓ yds. of print scraps (we used 3" strips from 16 different fabrics) for blocks

1¼ yds. of dark green print for sashing, inner border, outer border, and binding

½ yd. of medium brown print for setting triangles and middle border

⅛ yd. of gold print for hearts

1¼ yds. of fabric for backing

35" x 42" piece of batting

CUTTING INSTRUCTIONS

All measurements include ¼"-wide seam allowances. Cut the borders and largest pieces first, and then use the remaining fabric for paper piecing.

From the medium brown print fabric, cut:

    3 squares, 8½" x 8½"; cut squares twice diagonally to make 12 triangles (you will have two left over)

    2 squares, 5" x 5"; cut squares once diagonally to make 4 triangles

    2 strips, 1" x 30¾"

    2 strips, 1" x 24¾"

From the dark green print, cut:

    24 strips, 1" x 5"

    2 strips, 1" x 6"

    2 strips, 1" x 16"

    2 strips, 1"x 26"

    1 strip, 1" x 31"

    2 strips, 1½" x 28¾"

    2 strips, 1½" x 23¾"

    2 strips, 3½" x 31¾"

    2 strips, 3½" x 30¾"

ASSEMBLING THE QUILT

1. Using the Crazy Patch patterns on pages 36–37, transfer 6 Crazy Patch Heart blocks and 4 each of Crazy Patch block 1, 2, and 3 to the desired foundation material.

2. Refer to "Paper-Piecing Instructions" on pages 13–15 to construct the following blocks.

Heart Block
Make 6.

Block 1
Make 4.

Block 2
Make 4.

Block 3
Make 4.

3. Arrange the Crazy Patch blocks, Crazy Patch Heart blocks, 1"-wide green sashing strips, 8½" side setting triangles, and 5" corner setting triangles in diagonal rows as shown. Sew the 5"-long sashing strips between the blocks and at the end of each row, and then add the side setting triangles to the ends of the rows. Press seams toward the sashing. Stitch the rows of blocks and sashing together, adding the corner triangles last. Trim the quilt top to measure 21⅞" x 28¾".

4. Referring to "Straight-Cut Borders" on page 87, stitch the 28¾" dark green inner-border strips to the sides of the quilt top first; then stitch the 23¾" dark green strips to the top and bottom edges. Stitch the 30¾" medium brown middle-border strips to the sides of the quilt top; then stitch the 24¾" medium brown strips to the top and bottom

edges. Stitch the 31¾" dark green outer-border strips to the sides of the quilt top; then stitch the 30¾" dark green strips to the top and bottom edges.

5. Remove the paper foundations.

FINISHING THE QUILT

Refer to "Finishing Techniques" on pages 87–93.

1. Layer the wall hanging with batting and backing; baste. Quilt as desired.

2. Trim the batting and backing even with the quilt-top edges. Add a hanging sleeve if desired.

3. Make a continuous strip of binding totaling 145" (see "Binding" on page 90). Bind the edges of the quilt and add a label.

COLOR VARIATIONS

BE MY VALENTINE

Red hearts and cream backgrounds create
a wall hanging perfect for Valentine's Day.

BABY LOVE

Try changing the colors to soft pinks and
blues to create a cool-toned baby quilt.

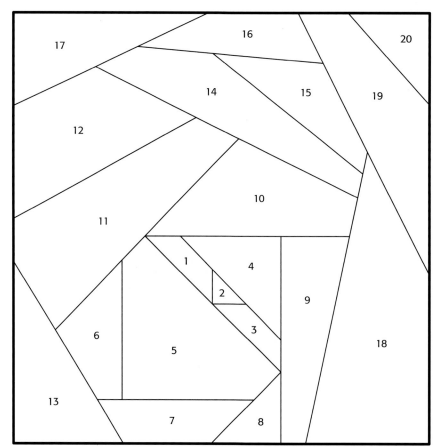

Heart Block
4½" x 4½"

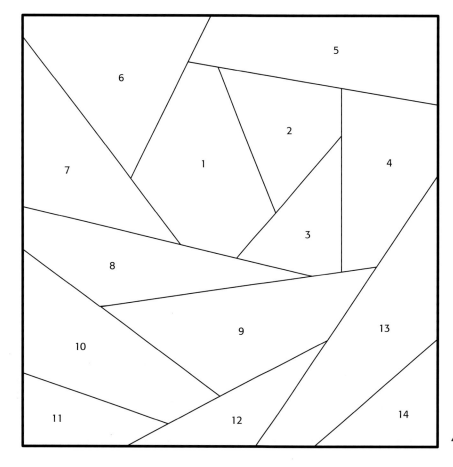

Block 1
4½" x 4½"

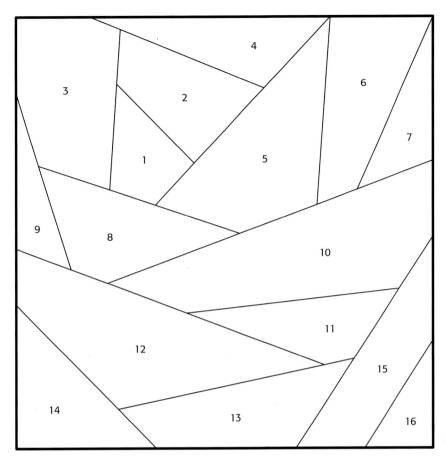

Block 2
4½" x 4½"

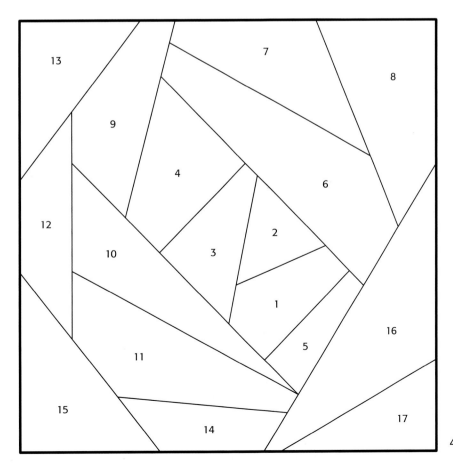

Block 3
4½" x 4½"

By Myra Harder. Quilted by Betty Klassen.
This project is a masculine design that comes from our design "archives,"
but it is still a favorite after so many years.

Hovering Hawk

FINISHED QUILT SIZE: 18" x 18"

MATERIALS

42"-wide fabric

½ yd. of gold print for background

⅜ yd. of green print for blocks and border

¼ yd. of black print for blocks and border

¾ yd. of fabric for backing

¼ yd. of fabric for binding or ⅓ yd. for stretcher-bar framing (see page 92)

22" x 22" piece of batting (24" x 24" for stretcher-bar framing)

ASSEMBLING THE QUILT

1. Using the Hovering Hawk patterns on pages 40–41, transfer 4 Hovering Hawk blocks, 16 border blocks, and 4 corner blocks to the desired foundation material.

2. Refer to "Paper-Piecing Instructions" on pages 13–15 to construct the following blocks.

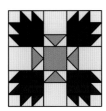

Hovering Hawk Block
Make 4.

Border Block   Corner Block
Make 16.   Make 4.

3. Join the 4 Hovering Hawk blocks as shown.

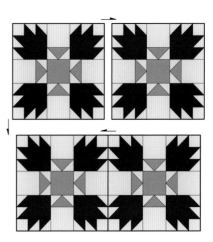

4. Join 4 border blocks as shown to make each of 2 side borders. Join 4 border blocks, adding a corner block to each end, to make each of the top and bottom borders as shown.

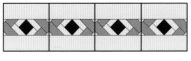

Sides
Make 2.

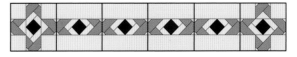

Top and Bottom
Make 2.

5. Stitch the side borders to the quilt top first, and then add the top and bottom borders. Press the seam allowances toward the borders.

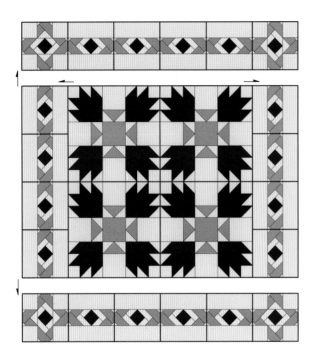

6. Remove the paper foundations.

FINISHING THE QUILT

Refer to "Finishing Techniques" on pages 87–93.

Frame the quilt as shown on page 38, referring to "Stretcher-Bar Framing" on page 92. Or, to finish with binding, follow these instructions.

1. Layer the wall hanging with batting and backing; baste. Quilt as desired.

2. Trim the batting and backing even with the quilt-top edges. Add a hanging sleeve if desired.

3. Make a continuous strip of binding totaling 82" (see "Binding" on page 90). Bind the edges of the quilt and add a label.

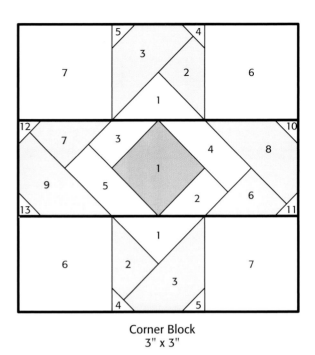

Corner Block
3" x 3"

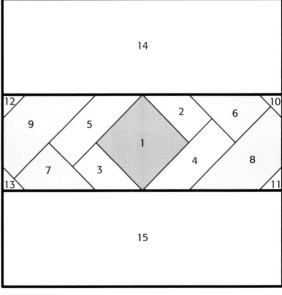

Border Block
3" x 3"

Hovering Hawk Block
6" x 6"

By Myra Harder and Betty Klassen. Quilted by Betty Klassen.
This design is one that evolved as we planned new and different projects for this book. This paper-pieced version of the Grandmother's Flower Garden design is much less time-consuming than the traditional method.

Grandma's Flower Garden

MATERIALS

42"-wide fabric

1¾ yds. of yellow print for border, blocks, and binding

1⅝ yds. of green print for blocks

⅓ yd. each of 4 different prints for flowers

¼ yd. each of 5 different prints for flowers

6" strip of gold print for flower centers

1½ yds. of fabric for backing

48" x 50" piece of batting

CUTTING INSTRUCTIONS

All measurements include ¼"-wide seam allowances. Cut the borders and largest pieces first, and then use the remaining fabric for paper piecing.

From the yellow print, cut:

 4 rectangles, 2½" x 2¾"

 2 strips, 5½" x 34½", cut on the lengthwise grain

 2 strips, 5½" x 46½", cut on the lengthwise grain

From the yellow print, green print, and 9 different prints for flowers, cut:

 180 rectangles total, 1⅝" x 2½", using the piecing diagram on page 44 as a guide.

ASSEMBLING THE QUILT

For this project every other horizontal row is paper-pieced and the alternate rows are pieced traditionally.

1. Using the Grandma's Flower Garden patterns on page 47, transfer 183 blocks to the desired foundation material. Twelve block patterns are printed on page 47. If you are making photocopies of the pattern, copy the page 16 times to get 192 copies of the pattern. Since only 183 copies are needed, you will have 9 copies left over.

TRADITIONAL PIECING

Early Grandmother's Flower Garden quilts are true treasures, especially when you understand that the hundreds of hexagons needed for each quilt were all pieced by hand. This long assembly process began with tracing each hexagon piece onto paper. The paper piece was pinned to the wrong side of the fabric, and then cut out from the fabric with a ¼" seam allowance all around. The next step was to fold the fabric back over the paper and baste it all around. The basting ensured that the hexagon corners would stay sharp and not become rounded. Once hundreds of these pieces were ready, the long task of hand stitching them together began. When the quilt top was finally assembled, the last step was to remove the paper pieces from the back of each piece.

2. Refer to "Paper-Piecing Instructions" on pages 13–15 to construct 183 blocks. Use the illustrations below and on page 45 as guides for fabric placement. Pay close attention when positioning fabrics since they will be pieced opposite of how they appear when finished.

Note: Some of the paper-pieced blocks along the outer edges of the quilt have piecing on 1 or 2 corners of the blocks only.

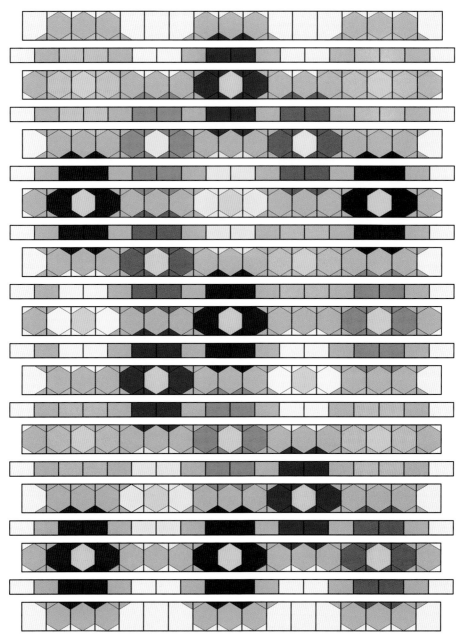

Piecing Diagram

3. Referring to the piecing diagram on page 44, arrange the paper-pieced blocks in horizontal rows, inserting the 2½" x 2¾" rectangles into the first and last rows as shown. Arrange the 1⅝" x 2½" rectangles in horizontal rows. Pay close attention to proper placement of the blocks and rectangles, so the colors line up accurately. Join the blocks and rectangles into rows. Join the rows, aligning for proper color placement (rows of rectangles will be longer than rows of blocks). Trim edges even along the sides.

4. Referring to "Straight-Cut Borders" on page 87, stitch the 34½" yellow border strips to the top and bottom of the quilt top, then stitch the 46½" side border strips to the side edges.

5. Remove the paper foundations.

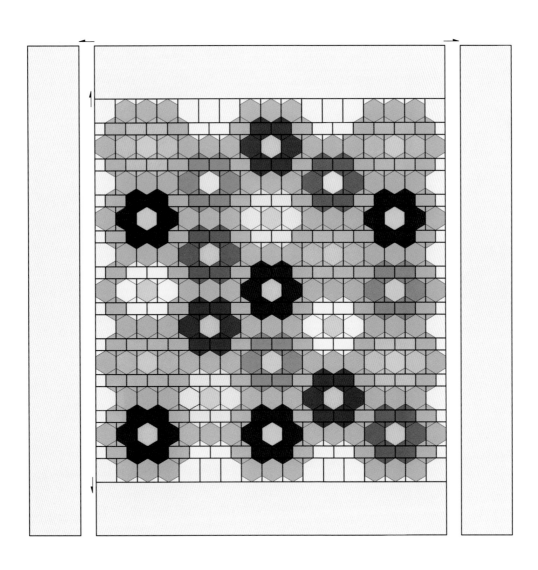

FINISHING THE QUILT

Refer to "Finishing Techniques" on pages 87–93.

1. Layer the wall hanging with batting and backing; baste. Quilt as desired.

2. Trim the batting and backing even with the quilt-top edges. Add a hanging sleeve if desired.

3. Make a continuous strip of binding totaling 190" (see "Binding" on page 90). Bind the edges of the quilt and add a label.

COLOR VARIATIONS

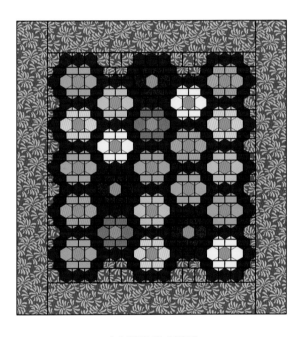

A NEW CLASSIC
Don't be afraid to try a bold print for the borders and bright colors for the flowers.

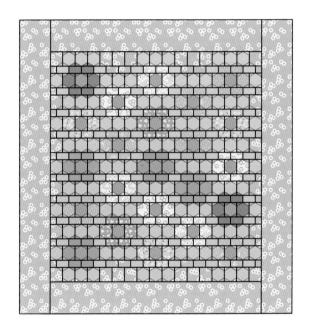

THE 1930s
This Grandma's Flower Garden quilt is the perfect place to use the 1930s prints in your stash.

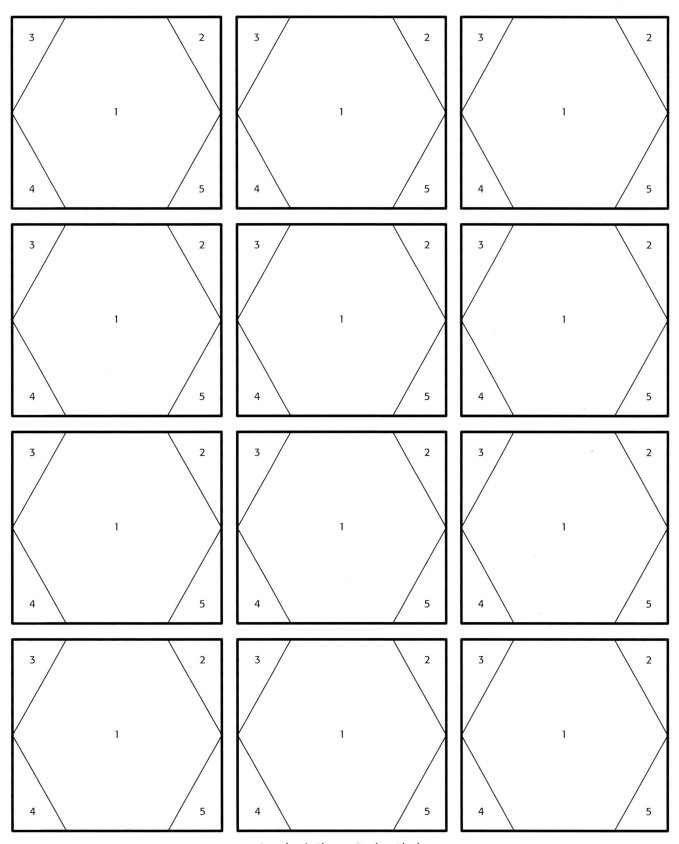

Grandma's Flower Garden Blocks
2¼" x 2"

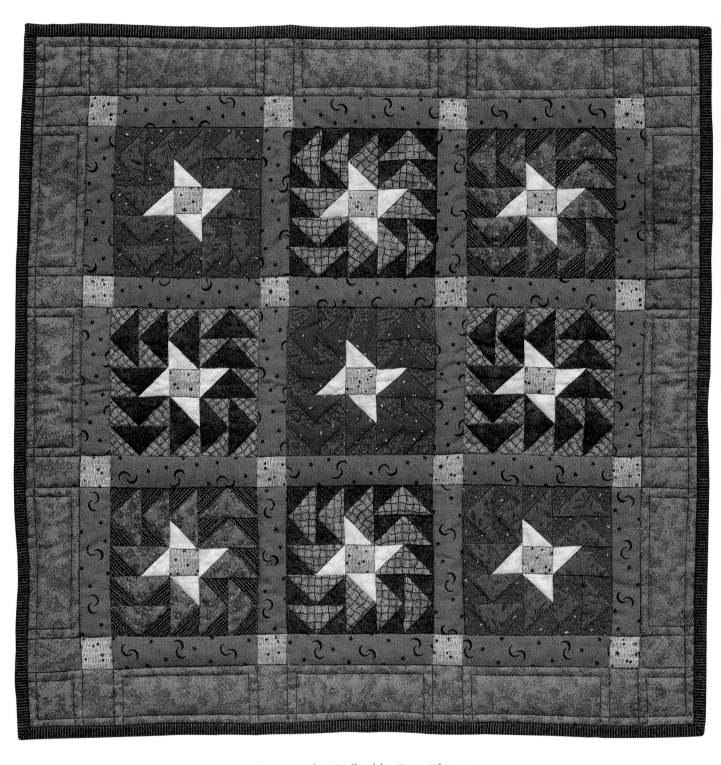

By Myra Harder. Quilted by Betty Klassen.
Flying Dutchman is a great little wall hanging for a special corner in your home.

Flying Dutchman

MATERIALS

42"-wide fabric

⅜ yd. of green print for outer border and flying geese in blocks

⅜ yd. of dark blue print for background of flying geese in blocks and for binding

¼ yd. of brown print for sashing and inner border

¼ yd. of green check for flying geese in blocks and for background

¼ yd. of dark red print for flying geese in blocks and for background

¼ yd. of dark rose print for flying geese in blocks and for background

¼ yd. of medium blue print for flying geese in blocks and for background

⅛ yd. of gold print for sashing squares, inner border, and star centers in blocks

⅛ yd. of yellow print for star tips

⅞ yd. of fabric for backing

28" x 28" piece of batting

CUTTING INSTRUCTIONS

All measurements include ¼"-wide seam allowances. Cut the borders and largest pieces first, and then use the remaining fabric for paper piecing.

From the brown print, cut:
    24 strips, 1½" x 5½"
From the gold print, cut:
    25 squares, 1½" x 1½"

From the green print, cut:
    2 strips, 2½" x 19½"
    2 strips, 2½" x 23½"

ASSEMBLING THE QUILT

1. Using the pattern on page 51, transfer 9 Dutchman's Puzzle blocks to the desired foundation material.

2. Refer to "Paper-Piecing Instructions" on pages 13–15 to construct the following blocks.

Make 2.

Make 2.

Make 2.

Make 2.

Make 1.

3. Arrange the blocks, 5½" brown sashing strips, and 1½" gold sashing squares as shown. Sew the pieces together in horizontal rows. Join the rows.

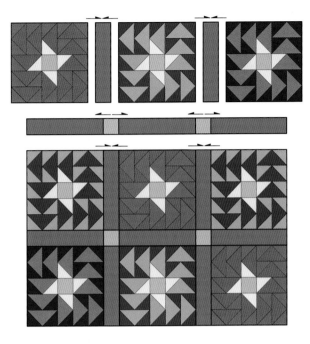

4. Join three 5½" brown strips and 2 gold squares as shown to make each of the side borders. Join 4 gold squares and three 5½" brown strips as shown to make each of the top and bottom borders. Press seam allowances away from the squares.

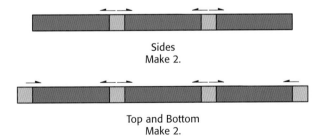

Sides
Make 2.

Top and Bottom
Make 2.

Stitch the side inner-border strips to the sides of the quilt top first, then stitch the top and bottom inner-border strips to the top and bottom edges. Press seam allowances toward the borders.

5. Referring to "Straight-Cut Borders" on page 87, stitch the 19½" green outer-border strips to the sides of the quilt top. Stitch the 23½" green outer-border strips to the top and bottom edges.

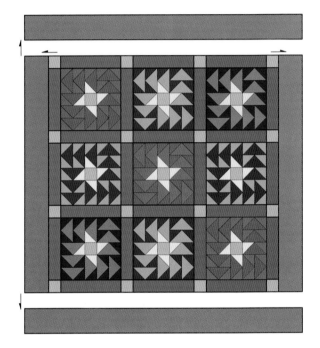

6. Remove the paper foundations.

FINISHING THE QUILT

Refer to "Finishing Techniques" on pages 87–93.

1. Layer the quilt top with batting and backing; baste. Quilt as desired.

2. Trim the batting and backing even with the quilt-top edges. Add a hanging sleeve if desired.

3. Make a continuous strip of binding totaling 104" (see "Binding" on page 90). Bind the edges of the quilt and add a label.

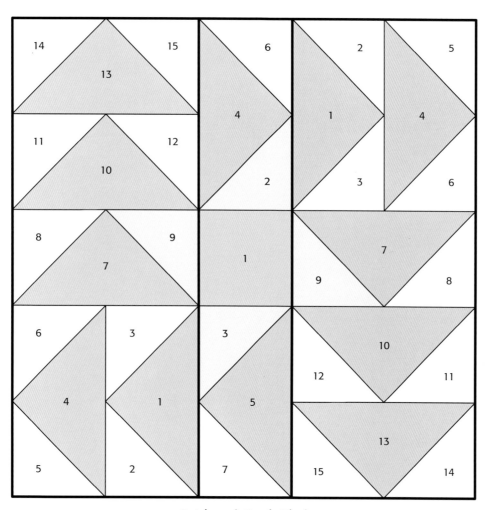

Dutchman's Puzzle Block
5" x 5"

By Betty Klassen

Myra has been a fan of Mariner's Compass quilts for a long time,
so it was inevitable that we would include one.

Mariner's Compass

FINISHED QUILT SIZE: 18½" x 18½"

MATERIALS

42"-wide fabric

⅜ yd. of blue print for background and middle border

¼ yd. of dark coral print for blocks and inner border

¼ yd. of coral print for blocks and outer border

¼ yd. of tan solid for blocks and outer border

2" strip of dark red print for blocks

2" strip of red print for blocks and corner squares

2" strip of gold print for blocks

¼ yd. of fabric for binding or ⅓ yd. of fabric for
    stretcher-bar framing (see page 92)

¾ yd. of fabric for backing

23" x 23" piece of batting (25" x 25" for stretcher-bar
    framing)

CUTTING INSTRUCTIONS

All measurements include ¼"-wide seam allowances.
Cut the borders and largest pieces first, and then use the
remaining fabric for paper piecing. Remember that
paper piecing produces a design that is a mirror image
of the pattern. Take care to position the fabrics correct-
ly for proper color placement in the finished quilt.

From the dark coral print, cut:
    2 strips, 1" x 13½"
    2 strips, 1" x 14½"
From the blue print, cut:
    2 strips, 1½" x 14½"
    2 strips, 1½" x 16½"
From the red print, cut:
    4 squares 1½" x 1½"

ASSEMBLING THE QUILT

1. Using the Mariner's Compass patterns on pages
   54–55, transfer 4 Mariner's Compass blocks and
   8 outer-border units to the desired foundation
   material.

2. Refer to "Paper-Piecing Instructions" on pages 13–15
   to construct the following block and border units.

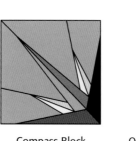

Compass Block
Make 4.

Outer-Border Unit
Make 8.

3. Arrange the 4 Mariner's Compass blocks as shown.
   Join the blocks into pairs, and then join the pairs.

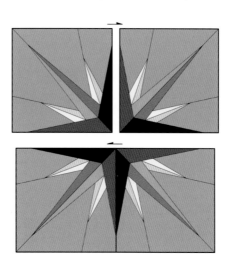

53

4. Referring to "Straight-Cut Borders" on page 87, stitch the 13½" dark coral strips to the sides of the quilt top first; then stitch the 14½" dark coral strips to the top and bottom edges. Stitch the 14½" blue print strips to the sides of the quilt top; then stitch the 16½" blue print strips to the top and bottom edges.

5. Join the border units into pairs to make the outer-border strips. Stitch outer-border strips to the sides of the quilt top first. Stitch red print squares to each end of the 2 remaining outer-border strips. Press seams toward the squares. Stitch the strips to the top and bottom edges of the quilt top.

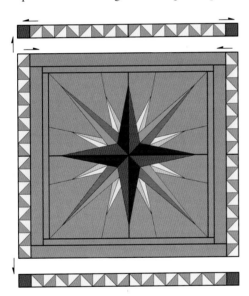

6. Remove the paper foundations.

FINISHING THE QUILT

Refer to "Finishing Techniques" on pages 87–93.

Frame the quilt as shown on page 52, referring to "Stretcher-Bar Framing" on page 92. Or, to finish with binding, follow these instructions.

1. Layer the wall hanging with batting and backing; baste. Quilt as desired.

2. Trim the batting and backing even with the quilt-top edges. Add a hanging sleeve if desired.

3. Make a continuous strip of binding totaling 84" (see "Binding" on page 90). Bind the edges of the quilt and add a label.

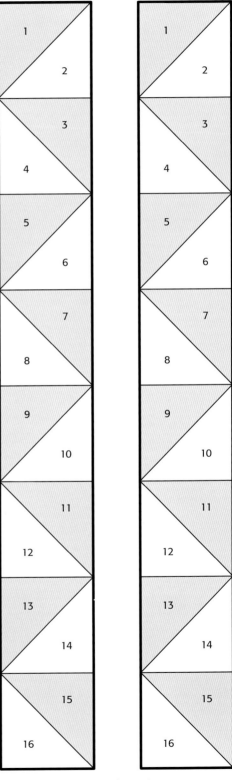

Outer-Border Units
1" x 8"

Compass Block
6½" x 6½"

By Myra Harder. Quilted by Betty Klassen.
The vintage spring colors and the re-creation of the flying geese
are a great combination of old and new.

Feathered Flying Geese

MATERIALS

42"-wide fabric

1¼ yds. of green print for sashing and border

⅔ yd. of dark green print for sashing, border, and
  binding

⅜ yd. of white for blocks

¼ yd. of peach print for blocks

¼ yd. of burnt red print for blocks

3" strip of yellow print for flying geese in blocks

3" strip of light green print for flying geese in blocks

3" strip of salmon solid for flying geese in blocks

1 yd. of fabric for backing

32" x 32" piece of batting

CUTTING INSTRUCTIONS

All measurements include ¼"-wide seam allowances.
Cut the borders and largest pieces first, and then use the
remaining fabric for paper piecing.

From the peach print, cut:
  4 squares, 7¼" x 7¼"; cut in half twice diagonally to
    make 16 triangles total

From the burnt red print, cut:
  4 squares, 2½" x 2½"

From the green print, cut:
  4 squares, 3½" x 3½"

ASSEMBLING THE QUILT

1. Using the Feathered Flying Geese patterns on
   pages 60–61, transfer 16 flying-geese units, 5
   sashing blocks, and 12 sashing units to the desired
   foundation material.

2. Refer to "Paper-Piecing Instructions" on pages
   13–15 to construct the following blocks and units.

Flying-Geese Unit
Make 16.

Sashing Block
Make 5.

Sashing Unit
Make 12.

3. Join 4 flying-geese units, 4 peach triangles, and a
   burnt red square as shown to make a Flying Geese
   block. Trim the block to 9½" x 9½".

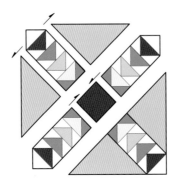

Make 4.

4. Join 1 sashing unit and 2 Flying Geese blocks to make each of 2 rows as shown. Press seam allowances away from the Flying Geese blocks.

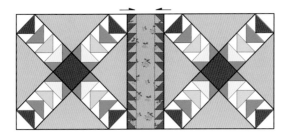

Make 2.

5. Join 2 sashing units and 1 sashing block as shown to make the middle sashing strip. Press seam allowances toward the sashing.

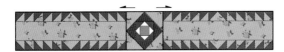

Make 1.

6. Join the 2 rows of blocks with the middle sashing strip between them. Press seam allowances away from the sashing strip.

7. Join 2 sashing units and 1 sashing block as shown to make the side borders. Join two 3½" green print squares, 1 sashing block, and 2 sashing units as shown to make the top and bottom border strips. Press seam allowances toward the sashing blocks.

Sides
Make 2.

Top and Bottom
Make 2.

Stitch the side border strips to the sides of the quilt top first; then stitch the top and bottom border strips to the top and bottom edges. Press seam allowances toward the borders.

8. Remove the paper foundations.

FINISHING THE QUILT

Refer to "Finishing Techniques" on pages 87–93.

1. Layer the quilt top with batting and backing; baste. Quilt as desired.

2. Trim the batting and backing even with the quilt-top edges. Add a hanging sleeve if desired.

3. Make a continuous strip of binding totaling 120" (see "Binding" on page 90). Bind the edges of the quilt and add a label.

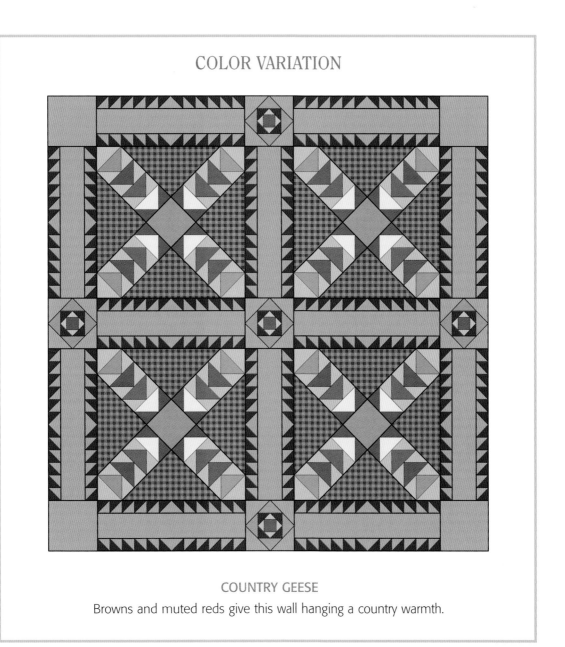

COLOR VARIATION

COUNTRY GEESE
Browns and muted reds give this wall hanging a country warmth.

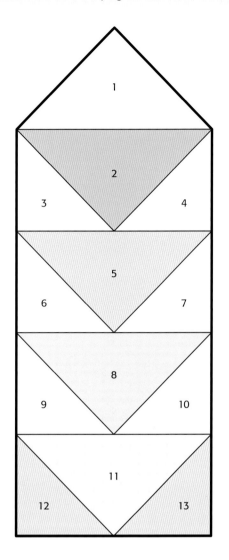
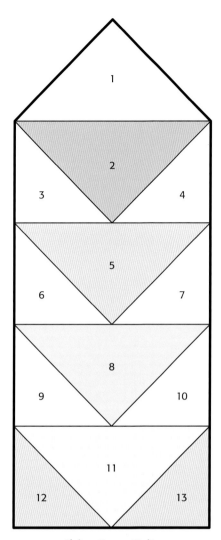
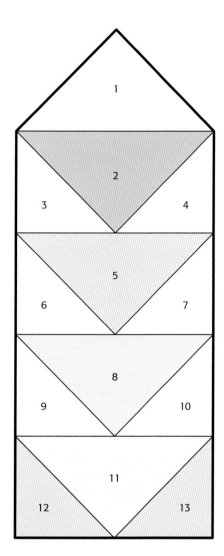

Flying Geese Units

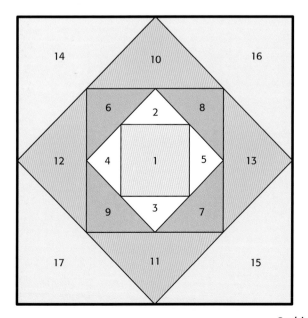
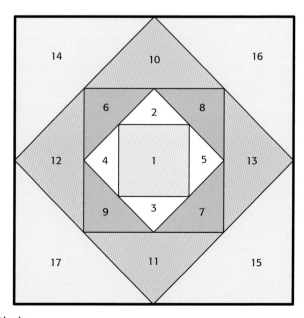

Sashing Blocks
3" x 3"

Sashing Units
3" x 9"

By Laura Kotschorek. Quilted by Betty Klassen.
The traditional schoolhouse teamed up with a touch of country is sure to bring you back to yesteryear.

Old Country School

MATERIALS

42"-wide fabric

⅞ yd. of cream print for background

⅞ yd. of red print for schoolhouses, corner squares, and binding

⅜ yd. of red plaid for outer border

⅛ yd. of khaki green print for fence

⅛ yd. of light yellow solid for windows and star centers

⅛ yd. of dark gold print for star points

1 yd. of fabric for backing

36" x 36" piece of batting

CUTTING INSTRUCTIONS

All measurements include ¼"-wide seam allowances. Cut the borders and largest pieces first, and then use the remaining fabric for paper piecing.

From the red print, cut:

16 squares, 1½" x 1½"

From the cream print, cut:

24 strips, 1½" x 7½"

From the red plaid, cut:

2 strips, 3½" x 25½"

2 strips, 3½" x 31½"

ASSEMBLING THE QUILT

1. Using the Old Country School patterns on pages 66–67, transfer 5 Schoolhouse blocks and 4 Fence blocks to the desired foundation material.

2. Refer to "Paper-Piecing Instructions" on pages 13–15 to construct the following blocks.

Schoolhouse Block
Make 5.

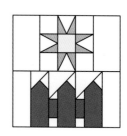
Fence Block
Make 4.

3. Join 2 red squares and three 7½" cream strips as shown to make each of 2 rows of horizontal sashing. Press seam allowances toward the cream strips.

Sashing Strip
Make 2.

4. Join 2 Schoolhouse blocks, 1 Fence block, and two 7½" cream sashing strips to make row 1; repeat for row 3. Join 2 Fence blocks, 1 Schoolhouse block, and 2 cream sashing strips to make row 2. Press the seam allowances toward the sashing.

5. Join the rows, adding the horizontal sashing strips between them.

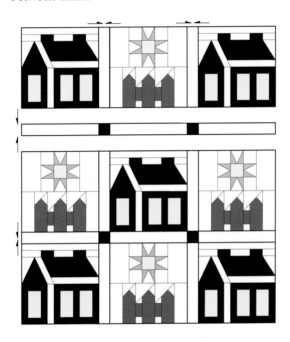

6. Join 2 red squares and three 7½" cream strips as shown to make the side inner border strips. Join 4 red squares and three 7½" cream strips as shown to make the top and bottom inner-border strips. Press seam allowances toward the cream strips.

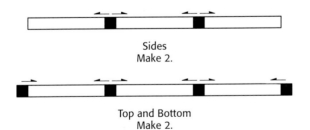

Sides
Make 2.

Top and Bottom
Make 2.

Stitch the side inner-border strips to the sides of the quilt top first; then stitch the top and bottom inner-border strips to the top and bottom edges. Press seam allowances toward borders.

7. Referring to "Straight-Cut Borders" on page 87, stitch the 25½" red plaid strips to the sides of the quilt top first; then stitch the 31½" red plaid strips to the top and bottom edges.

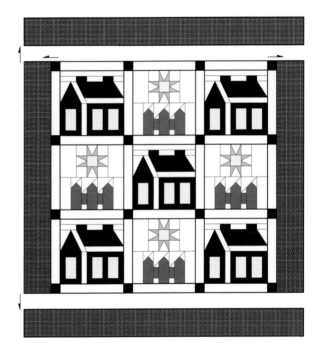

8. Remove the paper foundations.

FINISHING THE QUILT

Refer to "Finishing Techniques" on pages 87–93.

1. Layer the quilt top with batting and backing; baste. Quilt as desired.

2. Trim the batting and backing even with the quilt-top edges. Add a hanging sleeve if desired.

3. Make a continuous strip of binding totaling 136" (see "Binding" on page 90). Bind the edges of the quilt and add a label.

COLOR VARIATION

NIGHT SCHOOL
Change day to night by using a dark blue print as the background.

Fence Block
7" x 7"

Schoolhouse Block
7" x 7"

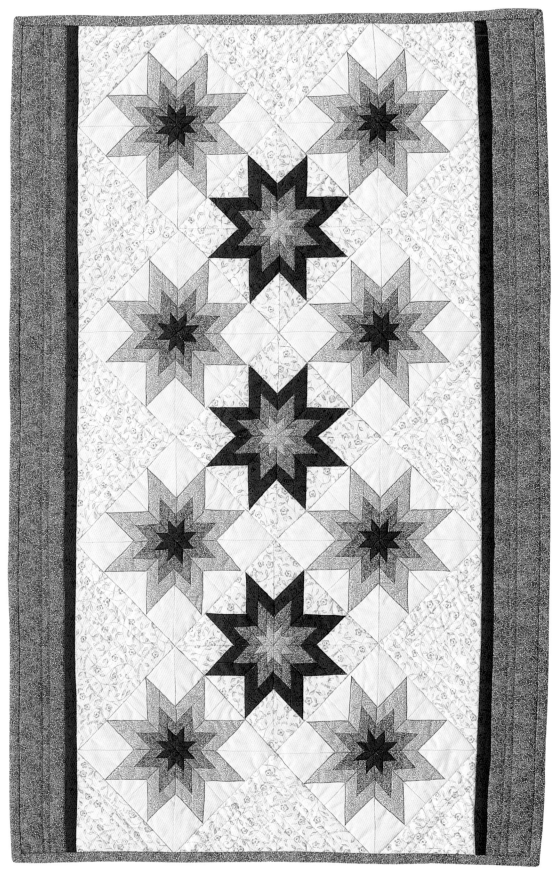

By Andrea Fehr and Pearl Braun-Dyck. Quilted by Betty Klassen.

In fresh colors of blue and yellow, this miniature collection of stars is sure to brighten up your home.

Lone Star

MATERIALS

42"-wide fabric

⅞ yd. of medium blue print for blocks, outer border, and binding

¾ yd. of yellow solid for blocks

½ yd. of light blue print for blocks

½ yd. of dark blue print for blocks and inner border

⅜ yd. of yellow print for background

⅞ yd. of fabric for backing

27" x 39" piece of batting

CUTTING INSTRUCTIONS

All measurements include ¼"-wide seam allowances. Cut the borders and largest pieces first, and then use the remaining fabric for paper piecing.

From the yellow print, cut:
- 2 squares, 9¼" x 9¼"; cut the squares in half diagonally twice to make 8 triangles total
- 2 squares, 5" x 5"; cut the squares in half diagonally once to make 4 triangles total

From the dark blue print, cut:
- 2 strips, 1" x 34½"

From the medium blue print, cut:
- 2 strips, 2½" x 34½"

ASSEMBLING THE QUILT

1. Using the Lone Star pattern on page 71, transfer 11 Star blocks to the desired foundation material.

2. Refer to "Paper-Piecing Instructions" on pages 13–15 to construct the following blocks.

Make 8.   Make 3.

3. Arrange and sew the Lone Star blocks, 9¼" side triangles, and 5" corner triangles in diagonal rows as shown. Join the rows, adding the corner triangles last. Trim the quilt top to measure 17½" x 34½".

4. Referring to "Straight-Cut Borders" on page 87, stitch the 1"-wide dark blue inner borders to the sides of the quilt top; then add the 2½"-wide medium blue outer borders.

5. Remove the paper foundations.

FINISHING THE QUILT

Refer to "Finishing Techniques" on pages 87–93.

1. Layer the quilt top with batting and backing; baste. Quilt as desired.

2. Trim the batting and backing even with the quilt-top edges. Add a hanging sleeve if desired.

3. Make a continuous strip of binding totaling 122" (see "Binding" on page 90). Bind the edges of the quilt and add a label.

COLOR VARIATION

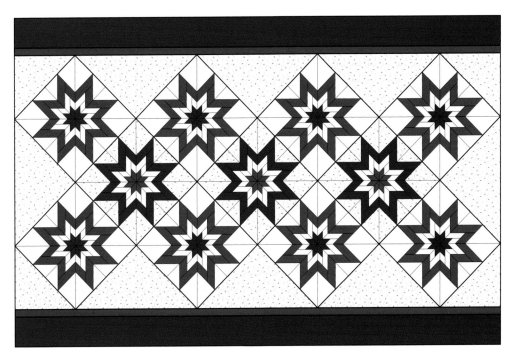

RED, WHITE, AND BLUE
This design lends itself perfectly to showing off your American pride.

Lone Star Block
6" x 6"

By Bev DeRoo. Quilted by Betty Klassen.
The ringlike appearance created by the combination of Amish colors
and blocks inspired us to name this project Amish Wedding.

Amish Wedding

FINISHED QUILT SIZE: 37¼" x 37¼"

MATERIALS

42"-wide fabric

1¾ yds. of medium green print for blocks, inner border, and outer border

1⅛ yds. of dark green print for blocks, inner border,
middle border, and binding

⅜ yd. of peach print for blocks

¼ yd. of medium purple print for blocks

2½ yds. of fabric for backing

42" x 42" piece of batting

CUTTING INSTRUCTIONS

All measurements include ¼"-wide seam allowances.
Cut the borders and largest pieces first, and then use the
remaining fabric for paper piecing.

From the medium green print, cut:

   12 pieces, 2¼" x 5¾"

   2 strips, 3" x 32¼"

   2 strips, 3" x 37¼"

From the dark green print, cut:

   2 strips, 1½" x 30¼"

   2 strips, 1½" x 32¼"

ASSEMBLING THE QUILT

1. Using the Amish Wedding patterns on pages
   76–77, transfer 12 Square-in-a-Square blocks, 13
   alternate blocks, 8 inner-border units, and 4 inner-
   border corner blocks to the desired foundation
   material.

2. Refer to "Paper-Piecing Instructions" on pages
   13–15 to construct the following blocks and units.

Square-in-a-Square Block
Make 12.

Alternate Block
Make 13.

Inner-Border
Corner Block
Make 4.

Inner-Border Unit
Make 8.

3. Arrange the Square-in-a-Square and alternate
   blocks into 5 rows of 5 blocks each. Sew the blocks
   together in horizontal rows. Join the rows. Press
   the seam allowances in one direction.

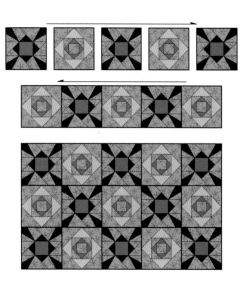

4. Join three 2¼" x 5¾" medium green rectangles and 2 inner-border units to make the side inner border as shown. Press seam allowances in the opposite direction of seam allowances joining rows. Join three 2¼" x 5¾" medium green rectangles, 2 inner-border units, and 2 inner-border corner blocks as shown to make the top and bottom inner borders. Press the seam allowances in the opposite direction of the row you're joining to.

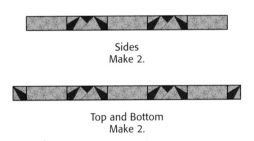

Sides
Make 2.

Top and Bottom
Make 2.

5. Stitch the side inner-border strips to the sides of the quilt top first, then stitch the top and bottom inner-border strips to the top and bottom edges. Press seam allowances toward the border strips.

6. Referring to "Straight-Cut Borders" on page 87, stitch the 30¼"-long dark green strips to the sides of the quilt top; then stitch the 32¼"-long dark green strips to the top and bottom edges. Stitch the 32¼"-long medium green strips to the side edges of the quilt top; then stitch the 37¼"-long strips to the top and bottom edges.

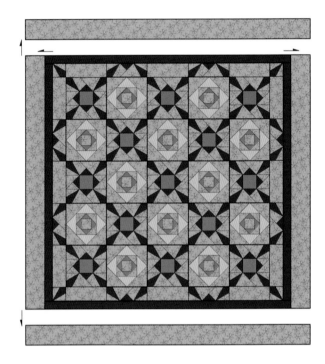

7. Remove the paper foundations.

FINISHING THE QUILT
Refer to "Finishing Techniques" on pages 87–93.

1. Layer the quilt top with batting and backing; baste. Quilt as desired.

2. Trim the batting and backing even with the quilt-top edges. Add a hanging sleeve if desired.

3. Make a continuous strip of binding totaling 159" (see "Binding" on page 90). Bind the edges of the quilt and add a label.

COLOR VARIATIONS

GARDEN RINGS

A simple change of background shifts this design from a traditional Amish look to a colorful garden treatment.

AMISH ALL THE WAY

To make this design even more Amish, simply change the background to traditional black and use solids in cool tones for the blocks and inner border.

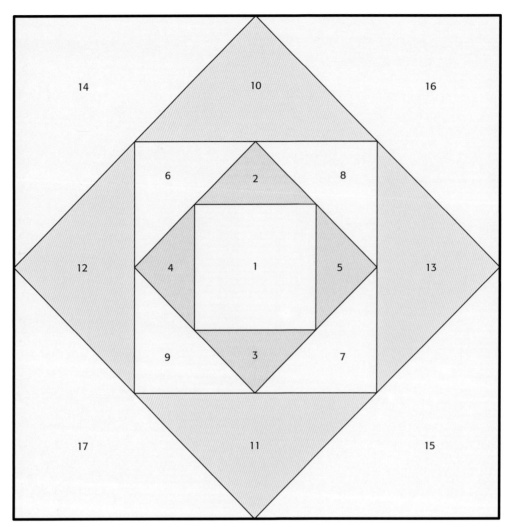

Square-in-a-Square Block
5¼" x 5¼"

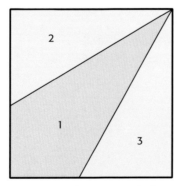

Inner-Border Corner Block
1¾" x 1¾"

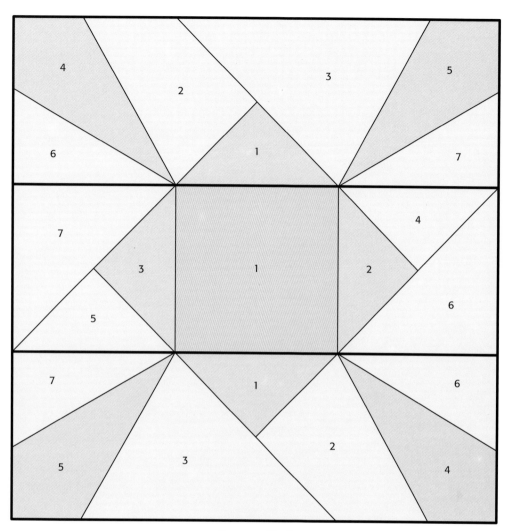

Alternate Block
5¼" x 5¼"

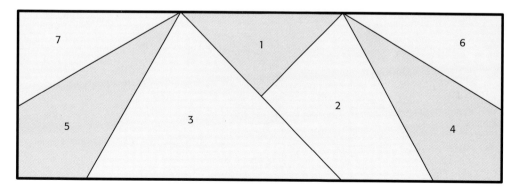

Inner-Border Unit
5¼" x 1¾"

By Andrea Fehr and Myra Harder. Quilted by Betty Klassen.
Fan quilts have always been popular with quilters;
we hope that you will enjoy this new twist on an old favorite.

Fan

MATERIALS

42"-wide fabric

1⅛ yds. of blue floral print for background, sashing, and binding

½ yd. of medium blue print for background

⅜ yd. of dark blue solid for blocks and sashing squares

½ yd. of light green print for blocks

½ yd. of medium green print for blocks

1 yd. of fabric for backing

34" x 34" piece of batting

CUTTING INSTRUCTIONS

All measurements include ¼"-wide seam allowances. Cut the largest pieces first, and then use the remaining fabrics for paper piecing.

From the blue floral print, cut:
    60 strips, 1½" x 4½"
From the dark blue solid, cut:
    25 squares, 1½" x 1½"

ASSEMBLING THE QUILT

1. Using the Fan patterns on page 81, transfer 36 Fan blocks to the desired foundation material.

2. Refer to "Paper-Piecing Instructions" on pages 13–15 to construct the following blocks.

Make 20.   Make 16.

3. Join 6 Fan blocks and five 1½" x 4½" blue floral print sashing strips to make each of 6 rows as shown. Press seam allowances toward the sashing strips.

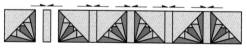

Make 2.

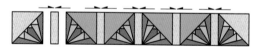

Make 4.

4. Join 5 dark blue squares and 6 blue floral print sashing strips as shown to make each of 5 rows of sashing. Press seam allowances toward the blue floral print.

Make 5.

5. Join the rows of blocks and sashing as shown.

6. Remove the paper foundations.

FINISHING THE QUILT
Refer to "Finishing Techniques" on pages 87–93.

1. Layer the quilt top with batting and backing; baste. Quilt as desired.

2. Trim the batting and backing even with the quilt-top edges. Add a hanging sleeve if desired.

3. Make a continuous strip of binding totaling 128" (see "Binding" on page 90). Bind the edges of the quilt and add a label.

COLOR VARIATION

GARDEN FANS
To add a touch of spring to your quilt,
try using a bright, cheery floral.

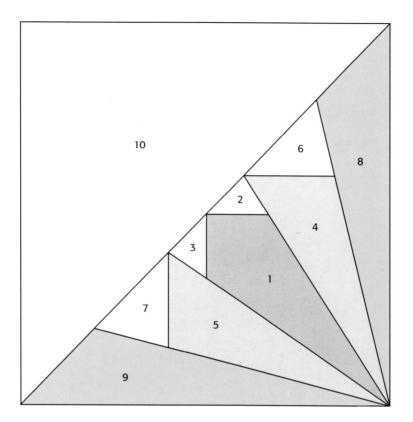

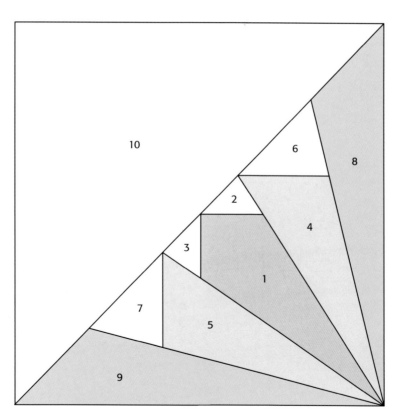

Fan Blocks
4" x 4"

By Cori Derksen. Quilted by Betty Klassen.
Fall is a favorite time for us, as we enjoy all the colors of the leaves.
It also reminds us that we need to get ready for winter, which will soon be here.

Leaves

MATERIALS

42"-wide fabric

⅜ yd. of medium green print for leaves, background, and binding

½ yd. of green print for setting triangles and borders

½ yd. of gold print for setting triangles and borders

¼ yd. of light green print for leaves and background

¼ yd. of dark orange print for leaves

¼ yd. of dark green print for leaves and background

¼ yd. of medium orange print for background

¼ yd. of dark gold print for leaves

¼ yd. of medium gold print for background

¼ yd. of light gold print for background

¼ yd. of brown fabric for leaves

⅞ yd. of fabric for backing

27" x 32" piece of batting

CUTTING INSTRUCTIONS

All measurements include ¼"-wide seam allowances. Cut the borders and largest pieces first, and then the remaining fabrics for paper piecing.

From the gold print, cut:

> 2 squares, 7" x 7"; cut the squares twice diagonally to make 8 triangles (you will have 3 triangles left over)
>
> 1 square, 3½" x 3½"; cut the square once diagonally to make 2 triangles
>
> 1 strip, 3½" x 23½"; cut the left end at a 45° angle
>
> 1 strip, 3½" x 21"; cut the right end at a 45° angle

From the green border print, cut:

> 2 squares, 7" x 7"; cut the squares twice diagonally to make 8 triangles (you will have 3 triangles left over)
>
> 1 square, 3½" x 3½"; cut the square once diagonally to make 2 triangles
>
> 1 strip, 3½" x 23½"; cut the left end at a 45° angle
>
> 1 strip, 3½" x 15¼"; cut the right end at a 45° angle

ASSEMBLING THE QUILT

1. Using the leaf patterns on page 86, transfer 21 Leaf blocks to the desired foundation material.

2. Refer to "Paper-Piecing Instructions" on pages 13–15 to construct the following blocks.

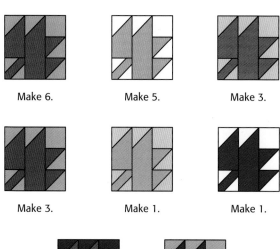

Make 6.   Make 5.   Make 3.

Make 3.   Make 1.   Make 1.

Make 1.   Make 1.

3. Stitch the blocks and 7" triangles into diagonal rows as shown.

4. Join the top 3 rows and then add the 3½" gold triangle to form the upper right corner. Trim the top and right side of the unit as necessary ¼" beyond the points of the leaf blocks. Join the 3½" x 23½" gold print border strip to the right side of the unit. Press seam allowances toward the border.

    Note: The remaining gold corner triangle will be added in step 7.

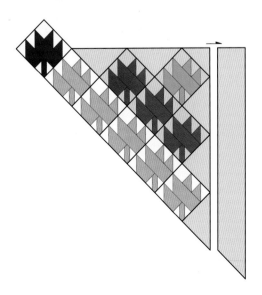

5. Join the remaining rows as shown, and then add the 3½" green triangle to form the lower right corner. Trim the left and bottom edges of the unit as necessary ¼" beyond the points of the leaf blocks. Join the 3½" x 23½" green print border strip to the left side of the unit. Press the seam allowances toward the border.

    Note: The remaining green print corner triangle will be added in step 7.

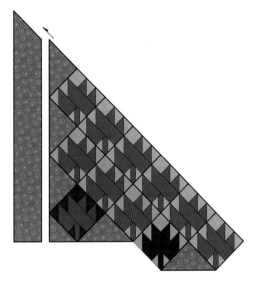

6. Join the top and bottom units. Pin the 3½" x 21" gold print border strip to the top of the piece, trimming any excess border length from the straight end, if necessary. Begin by sewing horizontally along the top, starting at the straight end. Stop sewing exactly on the seam line of the leaf block on the remaining end with your needle down in the fabric. Lift your presser foot and rotate the piece under the machine, lining up the angle of the leaf block with the angle of the border piece; pin in

place. Lower your presser foot and continue stitching along the angled end.

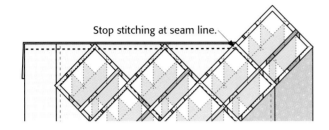

Stop stitching at seam line.

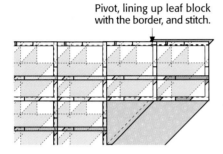

Pivot, lining up leaf block with the border, and stitch.

Join the 3½" x 15¼" green print border strip to the bottom of the piece in the same manner.

7. Add a gold print 3½" triangle to the top left corner of the piece. Add a green print 3½" triangle to the bottom right corner of the piece. Trim the edges of the corner triangles even with the edges of the quilt top.

8. Remove the paper foundations.

FINISHING THE QUILT

Refer to "Finishing Techniques" on pages 87–93.

1. Layer the quilt top with batting and backing; baste. Quilt as desired.

2. Trim the batting and backing even with the quilt-top edges. Add a hanging sleeve if desired.

3. Make a continuous strip of binding totaling 111" (see "Binding" on page 90). Bind the edges of the quilt and add a label.

COLOR VARIATION

BLACK, WHITE, AND SHADES OF GRAY
Changing the leaves to a monochromatic color scheme gives this quilt a very modern look.

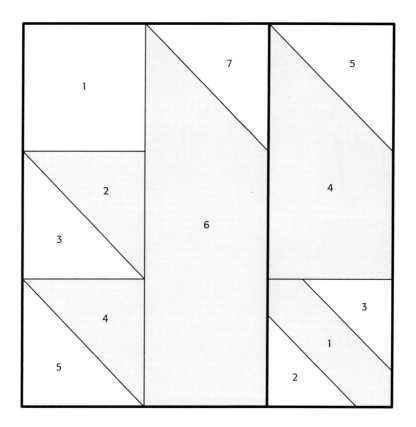

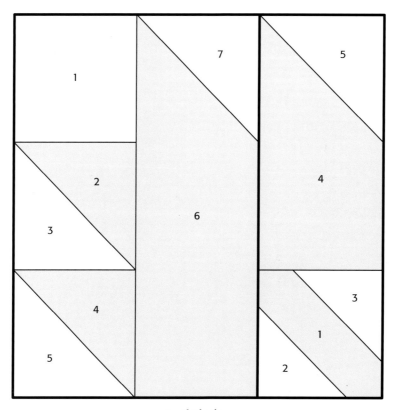

Leaf Blocks
4" x 4"

Finishing Techniques

Refer to the instructions in the sections below to finish your paper-pieced quilts.

ADDING BORDERS

Although specific border lengths are listed in the cutting directions for each project, it is best to measure your quilt top through the center in both directions before cutting border strips for your quilt. Cut your border strips across the width of the fabric and piece as necessary. You can avoid a seam by cutting long strips on the lengthwise grain line; however, additional fabric may be required. We typically add side borders first, and then top and bottom borders as indicated below. However, we decided to hang some of our horizontal wall hangings vertically after they were finished. For those, instructions are given for adding the top and bottom borders first, and then the side borders.

Straight-Cut Borders

1. Measure the length of your quilt top through the center and cut 2 border strips to that measurement, piecing as necessary. Mark the centers of the strips and the centers along the side edges of the quilt. Pin the strips to the sides of the quilt, matching the centers and ends. Stitch in place. Press seam allowances toward the borders.

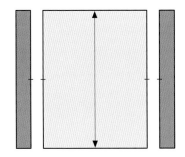

Measure center of quilt, top to bottom. Mark centers.

2. Measure the width of your quilt top through the center and cut 2 border strips to that measurement, piecing as necessary. Mark the centers of the strips and the centers along the top and bottom edges of the quilt. Pin the strips to the top and bottom edges of the quilt, matching the centers and ends. Stitch in place. Press seam allowances toward the borders.

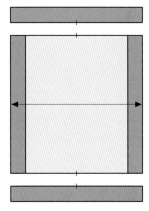

Measure center of quilt, side to side, including borders. Mark centers.

Borders with Corner Squares

1. Measure the length and width of your quilt top through the center and cut border strips to those measurements, piecing as necessary.

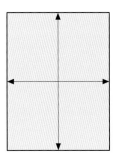

2. Mark the centers of the strips and the centers along the quilt edges. Pin the side border strips to the sides of the quilt top, matching centers and ends. Stitch in place. Press seam allowances toward the borders.

3. Cut or piece corner squares as indicated in the project directions. Stitch 1 corner square to each end of the remaining border strips; press seams toward the border strips.

4. Pin the border strips to the top and bottom edges of the quilt top, matching centers, seams, and ends. Stitch in place. Press seam allowances toward the borders.

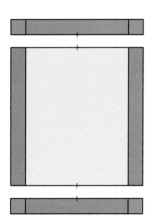

ASSEMBLING THE LAYERS

Once the quilt top is finished you will need to layer it with the batting and backing before you quilt it.

1. Mark the quilt top with the desired quilting design, if necessary.

2. Cut the backing and batting 4" larger than the pieced top. This will give you 2" extra on each side for the take-up that occurs during quilting. For large quilts, you may need to sew 2 lengths of fabric together and then trim away the excess to make a backing the required size.

3. Place the backing, right side down, on a flat surface. Using masking tape, secure it in several places along the edges. Make sure the backing is smooth and taut. Position the batting over the backing and smooth it into place. Center the pieced top, right side up, over the batting and backing.

4. Working from the center out, baste the layers together with thread or safety pins. Place safety pins 6" to 8" apart, away from intended quilting lines.

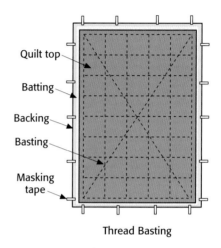

Quilt top
Batting
Backing
Basting
Masking tape

Thread Basting

Quilt top
Batting
Backing
Pins
Masking tape

Safety-Pin Basting

QUILTING

You can add quilting stitches to your quilt with either hand or machine quilting. Whatever method you use to finish your project, be creative and have fun with it! If you plan to frame your project with stretcher bars, see "Stretcher-Bar Framing" on page 92 before beginning your quilting.

Hand Quilting

We love projects that are finished with hand quilting; however, the many seam allowances created by paper piecing make hand stitching difficult. Limit hand quilting to quilts that have open spaces or use it in borders.

Machine Quilting

For most of our projects we used straight-line quilting, but we also chose channel quilting or outline quilting occasionally. Many of the quilts have in-the-ditch quilting between the blocks, sashings, and borders. A couple of the projects feature stipple quilting in the backgrounds, which helps to hide the seams within the blocks and also brings out the pattern. For best results, match the scale of the stippling to the design in the quilt. Another option is a curved quilting design, as shown in the blocks of "Feathered Flying Geese" on page 56.

ADDING A HANGING SLEEVE

A great way to display your quilt is to add a hanging sleeve to the back. We add sleeves to our quilts before we finish them with binding. It saves on hand stitching and produces a neat appearance.

1. Cut a strip of fabric 6" wide and 1" narrower than the width of the finished quilt.
2. Fold under each end of the strip ¼" and stitch in place.

3. Fold the strip in half lengthwise, wrong sides together. Baste the raw edges together to form a tube.

4. Center the raw edges of the strip along the top edge of the quilt back. Pin the sleeve in place.

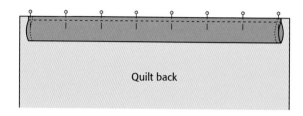

Quilt back

5. Bind the quilt as instructed in "Binding" on page 90, securing the sleeve in the seam.

6. After the binding is folded to the back and hand stitched in place, slipstitch the bottom of the sleeve to the quilt backing. Be careful not to stitch through to the front of the quilt.

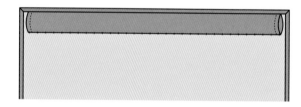

TIP To ensure your project looks its best and lies perfectly flat, mist your quilt from both sides and smooth it out with your hands. Then brush the entire quilt with a lint brush. Allow to dry.

FINISHING THE EDGES

Binding is the most common way to finish the edges of quilts. We occasionally use stretcher-bar framing to finish our quilts as well (see "Hovering Hawk" on page 38 and "Mariner's Compass" on page 52). Complete step-by-step instructions are given for binding your quilt on pages 90–91. We have included a description of the stretcher-bar framing technique on page 92 in case you want to consider this option. To use the stretcher-bar method, you will need to have a frame built especially for your project, or you will need to assemble a frame from artist's stretcher bars.

Binding

The binding that we are accustomed to using is often referred to as a double binding because it is folded in half before it is stitched to the edges of the quilt. We cut our binding strips 2½" wide across the width of the fabric. You will need enough strips to go around the perimeter of the quilt plus about 10" for seam allowances and mitered corners.

1. Cut the required number of strips to reach the binding measurement given for each individual project. To join the strips together so they are long enough to go around the project, place 2 strips right sides together so they are perpendicular to each other as shown. Draw a diagonal line on the top strip that extends from the point where the upper edges meet to the opposite point where the lower edges meet. Stitch along this line.

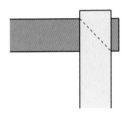

2. Trim the seam allowance to ¼". Press the seam allowances open. Add the remaining strips in the same manner.

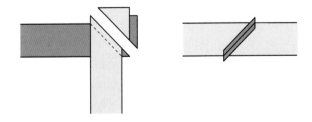

   When all of the strips have been added, cut one end at a 45° angle. This will be the beginning of the strip. Press the binding in half lengthwise, wrong sides together, aligning the raw edges.

3. Beginning with the angled end, place the binding strip along one edge of the right side of the quilt top. Align the raw edges and do not start near a corner. Leaving the first 8" of the binding unstitched, stitch the binding to the quilt. Use a ¼" seam allowance. Stop stitching ¼" from the corner. Backstitch and remove the quilt from the machine.

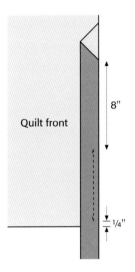

4. Turn the project so you are ready to sew the next side. Fold the binding up so it creates a 45°-angle fold.

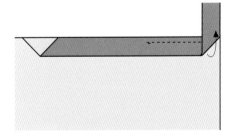

5. Place your finger on the fold to keep it in place; then fold the binding back down so the new fold is even with the top edge of the quilt and the binding raw edge is aligned with the side of the quilt. Beginning at the edge, stitch the binding to the

quilt, stopping ¼" from the next corner. Repeat the folding and stitching process for each corner.

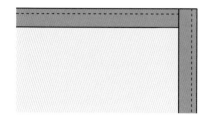

6. When you are 8" to 12" away from your starting point, stop stitching and remove the quilt from the machine. Cut the end of the binding strip so it overlaps the beginning of the binding strip by at least 5". Pin the ends together 3½" from the starting point. Clip the binding raw edges at the pin, being careful not to cut past the seam allowance or into the quilt layers. Open up the binding and match the ends as shown. Stitch the ends together on the diagonal.

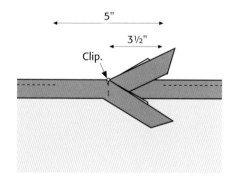

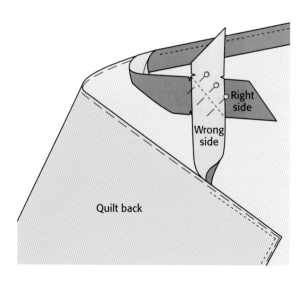

7. Refold the binding and check to make sure it fits the quilt. Trim the binding ends to ¼". Finish stitching the binding to the edge.

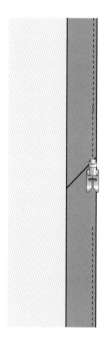

8. Fold the binding over the raw edges to the back of the project. Slipstitch the binding to the backing along the fold, mitering the corners.

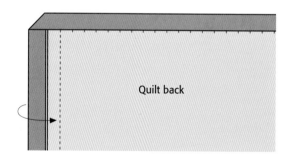

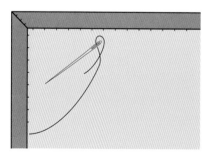

Stretcher-Bar Framing

To frame your quilt with stretcher bars, you will need to have a wooden frame built to the desired finished size of your piece. We have ours built from 1" x 1" pine boards. Pine is a good wood choice for easy stapling. We have the corners mitered and the front edge cut with an angled cut to produce a sharp edge. Anyone with basic carpentry tools can build this simple four-sided wooden frame. An alternative framing method would be to use artist's stretcher bars, which are available at art supply stores. They are sold in pairs by length, so you will need to buy one pair equal to the width of your quilt and one pair equal to the length of your quilt. If the artist's stretcher bars don't come in the dimensions you need, you may need to add an outer border to your quilt in order for your quilt dimensions to reach a size that can be accommodated by the precut stretcher-bar lengths. We recommend using the stretcher-bar framing method with projects 24" or smaller to prevent the boards from warping.

To secure your quilt top to either kind of frame, you will need to add strips of fabric to the sides and top and bottom of the quilt. These strips are added in the same manner as border strips. These strips are then wrapped around the edges of the frame to the back side and stapled in place. The fabric strips will show on the sides of the frame, so be sure to use a fabric that coordinates with your quilt top.

1. Lay the quilt top flat and determine the desired placement for the finished edges. Sometimes borders decide the edge and other times you may select the edge based on a design line in the fabric. Mark the position of your finished edges with pins. Measure the quilt top carefully in both directions between your desired finished edges to determine the frame size needed, and then have the frame built for you. Or, assemble artist's stretcher bars to the dimensions needed. Trim the quilt top to the desired finished size, adding ¼" seam allowances on all sides.

2. Referring to "Straight-Cut Borders" on page 87, measure and cut 3"-wide strips. Sew them to the sides of the quilt top first, and then to the top and bottom edges. Layer the quilt top with batting and backing; baste. Quilt as desired, leaving the fabric strips around the outer edges unquilted.

Add 3" framing strips.

Back of Quilt
Quilt the top only, leaving the
framing strips unquilted.

3. Lay the quilted piece face down on a flat surface. Place the wooden frame, front edge down, in position on the quilted piece. Mark the center along each edge of the quilt and mark the center on each side of the frame. Then, matching center points,

wrap the backing fabric around the edges of the frame and staple in place. Wrap the batting and quilt top around the edges of the frame and staple in place at the centers. The piece should feel tight, yet not so tight that the quilting is pulled flat. Continue stapling along the edges, from the centers out to about 5" from the corners. Staple the backing first and then the batting and quilt top. Stretch the piece as you go. Place the staples close together in both the backing and quilt top to avoid ripples in the fabrics.

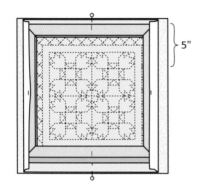

Staple backing at the center of all four sides, then to about 5" from the corners.

4. Trim the batting at the corners to eliminate bulk. Fold a 45° pleat to the inside to create a smooth corner. Staple in place. Continue stapling the backing, batting, and quilt top in place around the corners.

5. Trim excess fabric and batting close to the staples.

6. Add a picture hanger at the top center of the stretcher-bar frame, or across one corner if you want to hang the piece on point.

SIGNING YOUR QUILT

Your quilt is not finished unless it is signed. You may think this is unnecessary and a time-consuming step, but you will thank yourself for it later. As hard as we try, we often forget when we completed a project. So find yourself a permanent marking pen and make sure you write the following information onto a label:

⊛ Name and city of the person who made the quilt

⊛ The dates the quilt was started and completed

⊛ Any special occasion or reason for making the quilt

It will not take long before you will appreciate having taken the time to include this information on your finished project.

Carolina Lily
made by Myra Harder
and
Betty Klassen
quilted by Betty Klassen
Winkler, Manitoba, 2002

Featured in the book
"Traditional Quilts to Paper Piece"

About the Authors

Cori Derksen and Myra Harder

Together we established the Moonshyne Collection on February 14, 1997, when we casually started designing quilts and then began producing and wholesaling our patterns to stores across Canada.

In 1999 and 2000 two of our designs appeared in *American Patchwork and Quilting*. We could not produce the patterns fast enough, so this triggered the idea of a book. Our first book, *Down in the Valley: Paper-Pieced Houses and Buildings* was released by Martingale & Company in January 2001, followed by *All Through the Woods* in October 2001.

CORI DERKSEN

To tell you the truth, when I started quilting, traditional designs were not my favorite. As I have gotten older and more experienced in life and at quilting I have come to appreciate the things of the past. And here's another secret: I don't like projects that take years. I like to see results quickly, so the method of paper piecing teamed with the traditional designs was perfect. Myra and I have been designing together for about six years and, as we mentioned in the introduction, some of these designs are new and some are "old." We have spent countless hours in front of a computer screen designing and dreaming up new projects, revising and re-revising our older designs. Thus the concept of this book came about. We hope you enjoy the quilts as much as we do!

As I get older my appreciation for things changes. I hope that my children will appreciate the quilted heirlooms they will someday receive. Being a wife and raising two children, writing books, scrapbooking, and gardening keeps me busy—no, actually very busy! I am a stay-at-home mom pursuing a career that kind of fell into my lap. Having the support of my husband, Randy, daughter, Kierra, son, Lane, and extended family has been very important to me and I appreciate their support.

MYRA HARDER

Cori and I have been friends since kindergarten, when we were neighbors. Because we have known each other for such a long period of time, we each know how the other works, creates, and thinks. I have always been the one to jump in and start something, because I believe that Cori will know how to finish it.

I fought long and hard against my interest in quilting, but eventually the quilting bug did get under my skin. After high school, I went to work in my mother's quilt shop as the bookkeeper and even then I was able to ignore the quilting fever, until I convinced Cori to come with me on a trip to Lancaster, Pennsylvania. I had spent two years of my childhood growing up in the heart of Lancaster, and I always looked for a chance to return to see my good friends. By the time we left for the trip, the bug had already bitten Cori, and somehow I caught the fever right along with her.

Life as a wife and mother is very rewarding, but it can also be exhausting. When I get a chance at any free time, I love to spend it in the studio that my husband, Mark, built for me. It is a place all my own, where I can surround myself with countless books and an almost endless stash of fabric. My studio also contains stacks of boxes and binders where I file all of the sketches and drawings of quilts that may never get made. My passion is first studying the history of classic quilts and then creating my own designs. Thankfully, Cori comes along every now and then and organizes a bunch of sketches into a real book.

I live in Winkler, Manitoba, with my husband, Mark, son, Samson, and daughter, Robin. Together we enjoy spending time at the lake, visiting with friends, and just being together as a family. And if our Canadian winters are long enough, I may just find the time to make a quilt.

new and bestselling titles from

America's Best-Loved Craft & Hobby Books®

America's Best-Loved Quilt Books®

NEW RELEASES
1000 Great Quilt Blocks
Basically Brilliant Knits
Bright Quilts from Down Under
Christmas Delights
Creative Machine Stitching
Crochet for Tots
Crocheted Aran Sweaters
Cutting Corners
Everyday Embellishments
Folk Art Friends
Garden Party
Hocus Pocus!
Just Can't Cut It!
Quilter's Home: Winter, The
Sweet and Simple Baby Quilts
Time to Quilt
Today's Crochet
Traditional Quilts to Paper Piece

APPLIQUÉ
Appliquilt in the Cabin
Artful Album Quilts
Artful Appliqué
Blossoms in Winter
Color-Blend Appliqué
Sunbonnet Sue All through the Year

BABY QUILTS
Easy Paper-Pieced Baby Quilts
Even More Quilts for Baby
More Quilts for Baby
Play Quilts
Quilted Nursery, The
Quilts for Baby

HOLIDAY QUILTS & CRAFTS
Christmas Cats and Dogs
Creepy Crafty Halloween
Handcrafted Christmas, A
Make Room for Christmas Quilts
Welcome to the North Pole

HOME DECORATING
Decorated Kitchen, The
Decorated Porch, The
Dresden Fan
Gracing the Table
Make Room for Quilts
Quilts for Mantels and More
Sweet Dreams

LEARNING TO QUILT
101 Fabulous Rotary-Cut Quilts
Beyond the Blocks
Casual Quilter, The
Feathers That Fly
Joy of Quilting, The
Simple Joys of Quilting, The
Your First Quilt Book (or it should be!)

PAPER PIECING
40 Bright and Bold Paper-Pieced Blocks
50 Fabulous Paper-Pieced Stars
For the Birds
Quilter's Ark, A
Rich Traditions
Split-Diamond Dazzlers

ROTARY CUTTING
365 Quilt Blocks a Year Perpetual Calendar
Around the Block Again
Around the Block with Judy Hopkins
Fat Quarter Quilts
More Fat Quarter Quilts
Stack the Deck!
Triangle Tricks
Triangle-Free Quilts

SCRAP QUILTS
Nickel Quilts
Scrap Frenzy
Scrappy Duos
Spectacular Scraps
Strips and Strings
Successful Scrap Quilts

TOPICS IN QUILTMAKING
American Stenciled Quilts
Americana Quilts
Batik Beauties
Bed and Breakfast Quilts
Fabulous Quilts from Favorite Patterns
Frayed-Edge Fun
Patriotic Little Quilts
Reversible Quilts

CRAFTS
ABCs of Making Teddy Bears, The
Blissful Bath, The
Handcrafted Frames
Handcrafted Garden Accents
Handprint Quilts
Painted Chairs
Painted Whimsies

KNITTING & CROCHET
365 Knitting Stitches a Year Perpetual
   Calendar
Clever Knits
Crochet for Babies and Toddlers
Crocheted Sweaters
Knitted Sweaters for Every Season
Knitted Throws and More
Knitter's Book of Finishing Techniques, The
Knitter's Template, A
More Paintbox Knits
Paintbox Knits
Too Cute! Cotton Knits for Toddlers
Treasury of Rowan Knits, A
Ultimate Knitter's Guide, The

Our books are available at bookstores and your favorite craft, fabric, and yarn retailers. If you don't see the title you're looking for, visit us at **www.martingale-pub.com** or contact us at:

1-800-426-3126
International: 1-425-483-3313

Fax: 1-425-486-7596

Email: info@martingale-pub.com

For more information and a full list of our titles, visit our Web site.